This book doesn't make ~~sens~~ ~~cens~~ ~~scens~~ ~~sns~~ sense

(LIVING AND LEARNING WITH DYSLEXIA)

by Jean Augur

This book is dedicated to my three dear sons who were generous enough to share their experiences for the benefit of others.

ISBN 1 871458 00 5

Printed by Antony Rowe Ltd., Chippenham

Published by Bath Educational Publishers Ltd.,
7 Walcot Buildings,
London Road,
Bath. BA1 6AD

Contents

INTRODUCTION

*I consider myself to be in a unique position.
I am the mother of dyslexic sons and a teacher
of dyslexic children. I have had experience of
dyslexia from both sides of the problem.*

In this book I am writing about some of the experiences
I have had in both these capacities and I hope that the
things I have noticed will help parents and teachers.

I would like to make it clear that unless otherwise
stated, the comments are my own. Many of them are
my own personal feelings made through living with,
talking to, observing and teaching children who are, to
varying degrees experiencing difficulties which I regard
as dyslexic.

This is not intended to be a book for academics. It is a
simple, but I hope informative account, of my own
family — a family who live with dyslexia. Perhaps it will
answer some of the many questions which are asked of
me day after day by parents and teachers.

I decided to write this book because I talk to so many
parents of dyslexic children and to dyslexic adults during
the course of my work. Often they are worried and
sometimes unhappy people who have had a history of
failure. The histories are so similar, histories of difficulty
in learning how to read, being called lazy, stupid,
careless. Some are desperate when I see them because
they are unable to write legibly or spell accurately. Most
are relieved to find out that they may be dyslexic, and
not just thick. But what is dyslexia?

WHAT IS DYSLEXIA?

The definition recommended by the Research Group of Developmental Dyslexia of the World Federation of Neurology in 1968 reads:-

"A disorder manifested by a difficulty in learning to read despite conventional instruction, adequate intelligence and socio-cultural opportunity. It is dependent upon fundamental cognitive difficulties which are frequently of a constitutional character."

A more explicit definition is submitted in "Dyslexia Defined" by MacDonald Critchley & Eileen A. Critchley. It reads:-

DEVELOPMENTAL DYSLEXIA

"A learning disability which initially shows itself by difficulty in learning to read, and later by erratic spelling and by lack of facility in manipulating written as opposed to spoken words. The condition is cognitive in essence, and usually genetically determined. It is not due to intellectual inadequacy or lack of socio-cultural opportunity, or to faults in the technique of teaching, or to emotional factors, or to any known structural brain-defect. It probably represents a specific maturational defect which tends to lessen as the child grows older and is capable of considerable improvement, especially when appropriate remedial help is afforded at the earliest opportunity."

It is often easier to explain very simply to the person concerned that the reason for his difficulty is probably that one or more of the pathways to his brain necessary for reading and spelling has not fully matured. This gives him unreliable recall of words. He can certainly be helped by learning in a multi-sensory way, that is learning by the *simultaneous use* of eyes, ears, speech organs, fingers and muscles.

Many children are ready, and all their sensory pathways are integrating when they begin to read at school so they have very little problem. They can see a word, recognise it again for reading and recall it accurately when they want to write it down. The child who is weak in one or more of his sensory areas has poor recall and begins to fall behind in his development of language skills. Multi-sensory training strengthens the weaker areas while the child continues to work with his stronger ones. Nothing will stop him using his strengths.

I firmly believe that if all children in the reception classes were taught in this way the children who would normally read easily would not suffer but the child at risk would stand a much better chance of reading earlier. Spelling will be more difficult for him to acquire but he can have constructive help with this earlier, and need not begin to feel a failure.

TEACHING AND LEARNING

A good place to begin is at the beginning and as far as this book goes the beginning was when my teaching life began. When I left College, enthusiastic and feeling I was God's gift to teaching, I started my probationary year in a small old school which had originally been a Church. This was situated in a somewhat mixed but on the whole, fairly good residential area. There was a teaching staff of five including myself plus the Head-teacher, secretary and Welfare Assistant.

"DO YOU KNOW HOW TO TEACH READING?"
I soon discovered the Head was one who liked to get her priorities right and one of her first questions to me was "Do you know how to teach reading?" Why oh why did she have to ask that? Now, if she had asked "Do you play the piano well?" I could have said "Yes"; or "Do you know how to teach drama, dance, art, craft, P.E.?" I could have said "Yes" with conviction; or "Do you tell a good story?" I would have passed with honours, but "Do you know how to teach reading?" Well, I had to be honest. "I have had one or two lectures on it, but I've hardly any experience" I replied.

The truth was that my first teaching practice had been in a nursery school where reading was not part of the curriculum. The other two practices had been in schools where the class teachers had taken the opportunity of my being there to extract their poor readers for extra help and that left me with all those who could already read. I had certainly had no experience. Obviously used to such a reply from probationary teachers, she invited me into her office. I can't remember the exact conversation but this statement really stuck in my mind:- "In this area" she said "Look and Say" is the approved method of teaching reading." She checked with relief that I knew what "Look and Say" was. "However", she continued, "I like phonics and I want you to teach phonics as well as "Look and Say". With that combination you won't go far wrong." It appeared however, that with the Inspectors phonics was not so popular so she suggested I should not stress that side of it if we were unfortunate enough to receive a visit from them. There then followed an half hour session when the Head checked that I knew all the necessary sounds of the letters and with one or two helpful suggestions and the words "Now see how you get on" I entered my classroom and began my first day.

Somehow or other most of the children in my care responded to this, in my case somewhat haphazard system. Looking back on it, I think some of them would have learned to read whether I had been there or not. I know I often felt rather surprised when I found the children were reading, and I felt I was doing a splendid job with those who were "romping ahead" going from Book 1 to Books 2 and 3 and 4 and so on.

SOME HAD DIFFICULTY
There were naturally some who had a little difficulty and some who had barely started but this did not worry me too much. After all, I told myself, I had made a reasonable beginning and those who were not learning were probably the slow learners anyway. Some of them were younger and they had another two years in the Infant School. They would be bound to catch up and everything would be all right eventually. This is certainly

what I told their parents on open evening. "Don't worry" I was saying — me, with a whole year's teaching experience under my belt — "Don't worry he's young yet" or "He's immature" or "He's not ready to learn yet — give him time. Don't worry "it" will come." I suppose by "it" I meant reading. Heaven knows why I thought "it" would just come. Another favourite remark of mine was "Don't be so anxious, parents, you'll only make the situation worse!" In retrospect I don't think for one moment the parents I was speaking to were over-anxious. They were simply caring parents who wanted their children to read like the others who were going home saying "I'm on book 1 or 2 or 3 or 4."

I spent three very happy years in this school during which time I married. In due course my husband's work took us away from the area and I had to leave my job. Shortly afterwards our marriage was blessed with our first son Roderick and subsequently two more very welcome sons, Nigel and Christopher.

RODERICK

The next five years were spent among nappies, prams, puzzles, toys, activities, long walks, visits to the park, to the Zoo, watching Andy Pandy, reading stories over and over again, looking at picture books, colouring, painting, building with Lego, modelling, making sand pies, generally learning through all manner of experiences.

Knowing how many teachers feel about Mothers attempting to teach reading, alphabet names and sounds, I made no attempt to teach these things but felt quite sure that my first son would be "ready for reading" when the time came in view of the social background he came from, and the environment in which he had spent his first five years.

The day came all too quickly for Roderick to start School. He was not particularly impressed with it but seemed to have no complaints that I can remember, except to state that he hated going across the yard to the toilet.

The first year of Roderick's school life seemed to pass very quickly and apart from one or two odd remarks like "I wish my teacher wouldn't shout" and "I tripped over again today" seemed to be fairly uneventful. The only untoward thing I remember particularly was when the teacher asked the children to pair off with a friend. It was an art lesson. "Today" she said "You are going to paint your friend." Roderick and his partner took her statement literally and actually began to paint each other. He brought his painting overall home for me to wash and a little paint certainly goes a long way!

READING AT HOME

During this first year Roderick enjoyed looking at picture books but never showed any interest in reading at home. This didn't worry me too much. He'd probably had enough of it during the day at school, and I was determined he should not be pressed into reading at home. I continued to read to all three boys at some time during each day usually just before or after tea time, and at bed time.

Roderick may not have shown much interest in reading but he certainly showed great aptitude in the three dimensional skills and made the most intricate models out of building bricks, particularly Lego. He also gathered waste materials together such as cardboard boxes, the middles of toilet rolls, washing-up liquid bottles, and egg boxes. He made intricate forts, castles, engines and many other things out of them. Once Roderick found an old bed spring and a deflated football and in a very short time had transformed them into Zebedee from the Magic Roundabout. He also drew and painted very well, and spent many happy hours producing some delightful pictures and designs.

Towards the end of the first school year there was the inevitable open evening when my husband and I went proudly to the school to hear how Roderick had fared. We looked round the class-room and patiently waited our turn to speak to the teacher who on the whole, seemed quite satisfied. She told us that Roderick was a nice bright boy who spoke well and had a good vocabulary. He joined in with class activities, and answered questions intelligently. He made splendid models for the classroom and always had lots of pictures up on the wall.

"HOW IS HIS READING?"

Towards the end of the interview we asked the question all parents ask at such evenings. "How is his reading"? At this point the teacher was not quite so satisfied. The reading she had to admit was slow. Roderick couldn't seem to get the hang of it. He seemed to have a lot of difficulty remembering words and couldn't even remember them a few seconds after being told what they were. If he saw a word on one line and was told what it was, when he saw the same word on the next line it was as if he had never set eyes on it before. She admitted that she found this exasperating, and it was inclined to make her rather cross as she felt Roderick wasn't trying as hard as he should and was perhaps "lazy". This statement was unacceptable to us as we knew him so well and lazy he was not. He was a most persevering child who never gave up over anything. He was prepared to tackle anything, and if he found something difficult he would stick at it until he had overcome the obstacle or difficulty. It is the same now with a difficult physics problem. He will never give up. He goes on and on until he has cracked it.

REVERSED OR INVERTED LETTERS

"Is there anything else he has difficulty with?" we asked. Apparently there was. He had great difficulty copying writing especially from the blackboard, and his writing was "peculiar". He often reversed or inverted his letters and some days did mirror writing. As Roderick is left handed we decided between us that this might be the reason for the writing problem and as he matured the situation would improve. Anyway, as the teacher said, "It would come. He was nearly the youngest in the class and another year would make all the difference."

Those remarks sounded familiar! Surely they were the same words that I had used to parents all those years before — the parents whose children had not been reading very well — the children whom I had not taught to read. I felt a little uneasy but with the end of term activities and summer holidays coming, I pushed my thoughts to the back of my mind.

POOR CO-ORDINATION
The holidays arrived and we packed our bags and went off to find sea, sand and sunshine. School was forgotten for the time being. Holidays are meant to be enjoyed and this is what we intended to do. The family played ball games on the beach and I noticed particularly that Roderick still had difficulty throwing and catching a ball. He couldn't kick a ball either — it was as though he didn't know which foot to use and by the time he had made up his mind, the opportunity had passed. Cricket was almost a nightmare as he couldn't bowl straight and looked so awkward holding the bat in a left handed way. He was usually bowled out with the first ball. This was very frustrating to him as his younger brother Nigel, was so good at ball games. Roderick also continued to trip and fall a great deal and has some noticeable scars to prove it.

The holidays were over all too quickly. It was back to school for Roderick and his second year began. He was very lucky that year in having a teacher who in some ways would be considered somewhat old fashioned in her methods. Her class was run on structured lines and she did a great deal of formal teaching in a quiet classroom. She believed in the value of phonics and had much experience in teaching that way. She took time to teach good handwriting and to correct spelling. The quiet atmosphere in her classroom appealed to Roderick and it was particularly lucky for him that she happened to be left handed as he was. She was able to help him a great deal and even taught him to sew.

On the whole, school seemed to be going well. Roderick at last managed to teach himself to tie his shoelaces. There was no way he could do them in the way I did, that is by tying the knot, making a loop, wrapping the other end round and through and pulling it tight. Instead, he made the knot, looped the two ends and tied another knot with the loops. A much simpler method but just as effective. He later taught his brothers how to do this and now they all tie their shoes in this manner. The tying of his tie however still defeated him. Now, even at 19 years old he still cannot handle cuff links.

After Christmas Nigel began school and the Headteacher asked me if I had thought of going back to teaching on a part-time basis. In fact I hadn't thought of it before. I enjoyed being at home very much and had never for one moment missed teaching. My days had been happy and full and I was in no way anxious to be a career mother. However, it appeared there was a staff shortage and the Head asked me if I would consider helping out. As my mother and father had taken a flat near to where we lived and were prepared to look after Christopher, I decided that I would return part-time for a short time to help out until a permanent part-timer could be found. In fact I became the permanent part-timer and have been teaching ever since.

Although two of my children were attending the school in which I was teaching, I would not be teaching either of them and they seemed to be very pleased with the arrangements.

SPELLING WAS "ODD"

After I had been there for a few weeks Roderick's teacher asked if she could have a talk to me. It appeared she was worried about Roderick. She told me that he seemed to be gifted in so many ways but the skills which she felt mattered most, that is reading and spelling were most 'odd'. He couldn't seem to understand the idea of reading and spelling at all and was a real puzzle to her as he forgot everything so easily. He had great difficulty remembering the sounds of letters and blending them together and was having very little success with "Look and Say". His writing had improved a little but he just couldn't remember how to spell words. He tried to spell them phonetically but with only limited success and was continually mixing up b and d, p, g and q, n and u, f and t, h and y, s and z, for reading and writing. The teacher had made some notes to which she referred and told me that he read and wrote "was" for "saw", "on" for "no", "to" for "at", "from" for "for". One of the most peculiar things he had done however was to draw a lovely picture of the school and written underneath "ƨʞooɿ hw ƨi ƨiʜⱦ"(This is my school). It certainly was peculiar. I see this sort of thing every day now but then it was new to me and I had to confess I didn't understand it.

I was very grateful to the teacher for discussing Roderick's work with me, but we were both at a loss to know what to do about it. She informed me that the Head-teacher was going to have some of the slower readers to her room each day and she would like Roderick to go. Perhaps individual help was what he needed. I was sure she was right and we agreed to wait and see if there was any improvement. In fact, it seemed to make very little difference in spite of sympathetic and dedicated help. Roderick arrived at the end of his second and final year in the infants school reading very little and with very poor spelling. The second open evening arrived and the story was much the same as before. There were other things however.

TROUBLE TELLING THE TIME

Although maths was not too much of a problem Roderick had trouble telling the time. I had noticed this myself. He seemed to have very little sense of time and certainly couldn't use the clock. Quarter to and quarter past were all the same to him and he was totally confused about 3 o'clock and 9 o'clock. Looking back on his life, direction always seemed to be a problem to him. He confused "before" and "after", "yesterday" and "tomorrow", "forwards" and "backwards", "in front" and "behind". He would say "We went to see Grandma tomorrow". This didn't seem unusual at first but surely at seven he ought to be able to sort these things out.

Multiplication tables were a further difficulty. He couldn't remember them in order. The same applied to the days of the week and the months of the year, in fact anything that required sequential memory.

Nevertheless, this splendid conscientious teacher told me "Don't worry about these things. Roderick has only had two years in the infants school. He is obviously a late developer. "It" will come. He would have benefited from a third year." She felt sure he would be all right. I had great respect for the experience of this teacher and heard myself agreeing with what she was saying. Why was it then I felt so uneasy again? More remarks like the ones I used to make? However, Roderick didn't seem to be unhappy so I was sure there was no need to worry. We would wait and see how he got on when he went to junior school.

EYE TEST

To recap a little, during his time at infant school, Roderick had a school medical examination. All was well until the "eye test". He was given a shape to hold which looked like a capital E, he then had to stand a certain distance from a board with many such shapes on and turn his E to match the ones on the board e.g. E m Ǝ ш etc. As he found this operation somewhat difficult the nurse suggested that an appointment should be made for him to see the clinic optician who found Roderick to have what he described as astigmatism in one eye. It was not necessary for him to wear glasses, but he was to attend the clinic every six months for a check up.

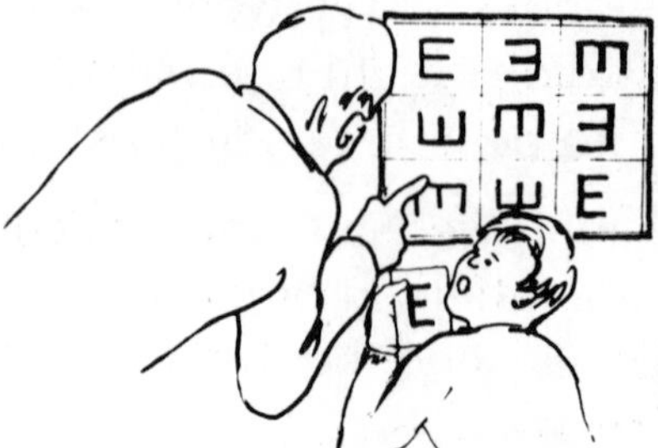

PHYSICALLY CLUMSY-MANUALLY SKILFUL

After the visit to the optician a thought suddenly struck me. Perhaps this astigmatism was the reason why Roderick often appeared to be so clumsy. He often bumped into objects, doors, tables, chairs, people, and had difficulty negotiating his own body through a given space. He tripped upstairs, fell downstairs, tripped over his own feet and this feature was particularly exaggerated when he was tired. He also knocked things over very easily — a vase of flowers, a bottle of milk, a jug of orange juice, which didn't help create the most peaceful atmosphere at meal times, which was when it often occurred. At this time I must confess that I referred to him as clumsy and found the situation rather exasperating. A table cloth could hardly ever be used more than once. We had to resort to mats on a formica topped table.

I couldn't understand why Roderick was so clumsy especially as he was so deft and competent with his hands. It just did not seem to add up. I was told that he was most ungainly in Physical Education lessons and always turned left when everyone else turned right or vice versa. However, with my usual optimism I was convinced it was a phase he was going through and it was bound to improve with time.

"HOW CAN I READ TO SING?"

With the summer holidays over, Roderick started at the local junior school. The first week was marred by a most unfortunate incident. For the first time in his school life he had been given a hymn book in assembly. One of the teachers noticed he was not singing and brought him out to the front telling him that he **must** sing in prayers. Whilst relating the story to me in the evening he said in a very sad voice "How can I read to sing, when I can't even read". For the first time since Roderick began his schooling I felt angry. Angry with a teacher who had shown so little understanding, and in that one morning had made assembly a very unpleasant start to the day when it should have been such a pleasure. I have a feeling it was about this time Roderick decided two things — one was that he was going to conquer this reading business which everyone else seemed to manage. The other was, that while he was conquering it, he would devise tactical methods of dealing with the problems like pretending to sing in prayers by just opening and closing his mouth at what he hoped were the appropriate places.

During this first junior school year Roderick won an art prize in a competition for National Library Week. This was a great boost to his morale but the prize was a

Book Token. What a disappointment. As far as Roderick was concerned, books were very low on his list of priorities. He would much rather have had paints or crayons or Lego. After much searching he finally found a selection of books which he exchanged for the token. It was some time however, before he opened them, and a good deal longer before he read them.

SHEER GUTS — PLUS PADDINGTON BEAR

When the time came for us to meet the teacher at the end of the year she seemed to think Roderick had had a fairly good year, nothing outstanding but he had settled down fairly well. She thought he wasn't particularly bright but he tried hard and was no bother. When I asked my usual question — in fact the question most parents ask — "What about his reading?" she replied that there was no problem. I was rather surprised at this and said "But he's hardly reading at all". "Oh isn't he?" she said, "We don't hear them read individually very often in the junior school." However, she promised to look into the matter and see what could be done. She was as good as her word. She informed the teacher Roderick was to have the following year and with her help and Roddy's sheer guts and determination, he certainly began to read albeit very slowly.

Thank goodness for the arrival of Paddington Bear. Roderick was given a Paddington Bear book for Christmas when he was 8½ years old and very slowly read it from cover to cover really enjoying reading for the first time. Having done so, he bought another, and another and another. He really seemed to be enjoying reading at last. In fact he seemed to improve all round apart from very very poor spelling which in my innocence, or ignorance, I thought would improve as he read more. It amazed me that he could recognise many words now for reading but couldn't recall them if he needed them for spelling, even the smallest words. Consequently, he was always having to do a great many spelling corrections. His attempts to find words in the dictionary ended in temper and tears and with the words "Dictionaries are stupid — you have to know how to spell the silly word in order to look up how to spell it." If only I knew then what I know now, how much and how easily I could have helped him.

"THIS BOOK IS STUPID!"
By this time, the amount of reading and writing Roderick was required to do was increasing. Although Paddington Bear was going well, there were many books which were much too difficult for him. He would misread constantly and often misunderstand the meaning. His constant cry was "This book is stupid — it doesn't make sense" — and of course it didn't to Roderick who was constantly reversing, transposing, omitting and inserting letters and words. He had another saying at this time. He often had great difficulty remembering certain words when writing or relating a story and would say "the word escapes me". This used to make him extremely annoyed — he found it most frustrating. Very often by a lengthy process

of elimination, or as he used to call it illumination, between us we finally hit on the elusive word. He couldn't rest until this had been achieved. One day when we were alone he said to me "Do you know what I think?" "What's that?" I replied. "I think God's put my brain in upside down!" It certainly must have appeared like that to a boy who always appeared to be seeing things wrongly.

Misreading of course, happens to everyone occasionally, but it's not just occasionally for the dyslexic. It is a daily or even hourly hazard. The dyslexic must concentrate every second and be prepared to read his text two or three times to be perfectly sure of it. This is particularly important in examinations and that is why extra time should be allowed for extra careful reading of the questions and to give time at the end for proof reading.

READING ALOUD
Reading aloud was and still is a very difficult thing for Roderick to do as he often misreads the words and entirely alters the meaning of the text. I remember one morning he was looking at the newspaper and he commented on a certain headline over the account of a particularly horrifying train accident. "Oh" said Roderick "the Queen is going to give blood. Isn't that splendid of her?" On checking the headline it said:-
"QUEUE TO GIVE BLOOD" not "QUEEN TO GIVE BLOOD"
A similar instance was when a group of business men were going to a conference in America. The newspaper reported that the spokesman had stated "We are going to exchange VIEWS with our American colleagues. Roderick totally mis-read this as "We are going to exchange WIVES with our American colleagues. Quite a different type of conference!

'BEARDED FISH'!

One day when we were shopping in the local supermarket Roderick asked "What is bearded fish?" I don't think there is any such thing" I replied. "Oh yes there is" said Roderick "It's sold here." He pointed to a notice on the fish counter which said "BREADED FISH". Looking at my face he said "I've done it again haven't I?" I often feel it was at this point that Roderick made up his mind that he would have to look twice at every word if he was to be absolutely sure he had read it correctly. This is one of the reasons why reading is still a fairly laborious business for him even now. He never leaves anything to chance and has developed a thoroughness in his approach to work which is probably one of the reasons for his success.

DYSLEXICS HATE TO BE LAUGHED AT

This misreading of course, especially when it is out loud, is the reason why dyslexics often become the class comedians. Their peers laugh at their mistakes which often do sound very funny. The dyslexic hates to be laughed at, but he dare not cry so he laughs with the class — better to join in the laughter even if it hurts.

To return to Roderick's school life — he had settled down fairly well and I really began to think his troubles were nearly over. His reports always commended him highly for his efforts but were always accompanied by comments such as:-

"He needs to work hard at his spelling."
"Lacks confidence when reading."
"Could do better work with more concentration."
"Good orally."
"Tends to dream instead of work."

For the last two years of his junior school Roderick was

taught by an excellent male teacher — one who had a formal and structured approach to teaching which suited Roderick very well. He thrived in this environment. At 11+ he was offered a Grammar School place — he really had made up for lost time. After discussion with Roderick, my husband and I decided not to accept the Grammar School place but to send him to a new Church of England Secondary School which we felt would be the best place for Roderick to spend his secondary school years. This school was organised on comprehensive lines and we felt that Roderick would not be pressured academically there. He would be able to proceed at his own pace and have plenty of scope to pursue his practical talents in an environment which, it was hoped would be sympathetic if any problems arose.

MOMENT OF TRUTH

Shortly before Roderick started secondary school I had seen purely by chance on television a programme about a boy of Roderick's age who had similar problems. In fact, the boy could have been Roderick and for the first time I heard the word dyslexia. From then on I read everything I could lay my hands on which would enlighten me on this subject but I kept my thoughts to myself. Roderick must be over it anyway, and I was convinced everything would be fine from now on. After all he was getting older and maturing all the time.

My hopes were short lived. The change from junior school to secondary school can be a fairly traumatic experience for some children but I hadn't appreciated the sort of difficulties we began to encounter. Roderick had been within walking distance of both his infant and junior schools but now for the first time he had to make a journey to school on public transport. There were several routes Roderick could take, and although the distance was only a few miles it was an awkward journey on public transport. He tried the various routes during the summer holiday and finally settled on the one he preferred. I could have taken him quite easily by car but not wishing to be an over-protective mother, I decided against it. His route required a walk to the bus-stop and a bus journey of three or four miles after which he alighted and caught a train for a short journey. The school was then about five minutes walk from the station. I simply hadn't realised how tiring this return journey would be for a boy who had to concentrate so hard during the day. By the time he got home he was really exhausted. He then had to start on his homework which often took a very long time. By the end of the first week he was thoroughly fatigued and not very happy.

ALWAYS GETTING LOST

Although not a large school by comparison with others, Roderick could not find his way around the building. The geography of the building mystified him. He was always getting lost, frequently late for lessons, and consequently getting into trouble. He was late changing back from Physical Education and could never tie his tie and his shoe laces quickly enough. The whole business of hurrying from one place to another was totally confusing.

One afternoon I decided to go and meet Roderick in the car but he was very late coming out. When he finally did emerge, he was white faced and near to tears. This was most unlike him. He was unable to speak at first, but when he did finally find his tongue it was to say that he had every intention of reporting a particular teacher to the N.S.P.C.C. On the way home the story unfolded.

HUMILIATION

Roderick had until this moment been fascinated and thrilled by science but had had a rather distressing experience in the science lesson on this particular day. It appeared that many objects had been placed all round the room and the children had to go round feeling, smelling and looking at them all, and then write down their findings. Roderick had quickly made his observations but then found the writing down of his information very difficult and succeeded in achieving very little. The little written work he had done was poorly spelt and the teacher was not at all pleased. Unfortunately he had humiliated Roderick in front of the class calling him lazy and careless. Children forgive a great deal but find ridicule and injustice hard to bear. If only this teacher had realised Roderick's difficulty and asked him to explain his findings instead of writing them down, he would have quickly realised the boy was in no way lazy or careless.

It was at this stage I decided I must explain to the Head of the school exactly what were the things Roderick found difficult so I telephoned for an appointment. A date was offered immediately and my husband and I met the Headmaster. I explained the problem and took examples of Roderick's work. The Head listened with great interest but had to admit the problem was new to him. However, he promised to pass on the information to the staff explaining the difficulties Roderick was having in written language, asking them to be patient and treat him with understanding. After this Roderick seemed to settle down a little better. He still found the written work hard, homework took him far too long, he was in total confusion with French and his English spelling was peculiar, even bizarre at times. Reading was laboured, note-taking difficult, and he had a great many tripping and falling accidents during the first two terms. Gradually towards the end of the first academic year he settled down and once again I felt that the problems were sorting themselves out. The staff in the main tried to understand and appreciated the amount of effort he made. They helped and supported him and on the whole I was well pleased. I say "on the whole" because there was an incident which sticks in my mind as being rather unfortunate.

PAINSTAKING

Roderick together with other boys had been mis-behaving in class and was given an essay to write on 'manners'. This was a week-end assignment. I insisted that the essay should be done well. I didn't object to the punishment, as such, even though I knew it was a demanding one for Roderick.

We discussed the subject of manners, did a rough plan with a beginning, middle and conclusion and then Roderick painstakingly wrote his essay. We read it through together when it was finished. The content was good, the handwriting neat, and he had tried hard with the spelling. He was well pleased with it. The punishment had been completed. On Monday Roderick took the essay to school and handed it to the teacher who promptly tore it up in front of his face without even looking at it. That man lost all respect Roderick had previously had for him. If only he had known the effort which had gone into that punishment. I felt ashamed of my profession.

INCREASED THE PROBLEM

Although that piece of work so deserved to be read but wasn't, it was not such a waste of time as some punishments I have known, punishments which have not only been useless but positively damaging for a dyslexic child such as copying a page out of a telephone directory. Copying is such a difficult activity for the dyslexic who finds it extremely exhausting to copy accurately one line, let alone a whole page. Another favoured punishment is to give lines. I saw this once with a child who had written "I must behav in clas". The child might have benefited in some way if the words had been spelt correctly but to write "behave" and "class" wrongly one hundred times could only have increased his spelling problem.

Although not a punishment another recent innovation which seems to be very popular at the moment and fills me with horror is the "sponsored spell". Admittedly it raises funds for charity but is very hard on a child who finds spelling difficult. Usually the idea is to present the child with a hundred words which he is supposed to learn and ask people to sponsor him so much a word for each correct spelling. It must be quite fun for the child with no spelling problems but very hard on others.

Roderick's first year at secondary school was drawing to a close and in spite of all his hard work examination results were not as good as he hoped. The report bore remarks such as "Roderick has worked steadily and well. Unfortunately in the stress of his examinations he failed badly in accuracy". "Roderick is a conscientious pupil which unfortunately was not properly reflected in his results from the recent examinations".

'TOPSY-TURVY DAYS'

Yet Roderick is a fighter — he never gives up and so far his story is one of success. He went on to take 7 O levels, and a C.S.E. in French, all with excellent grades. He spent two years in the sixth form, succeeded in getting A levels in Physics, Chemistry and Mathematics all with top grades and is now reading Physics at Imperial College, University of London. Over the years he has suffered bouts of absolute exhaustion particularly at the end of a term or after doing exams and he still has days when everything goes wrong for him, usually when he is tired or sickening for a cold, or as recently in an attack of glandular fever. These are the days when he severely mis-reads and mis-spells, and still trips up and down stairs and bumps into things. These are usually referred to in the family as the Topsy-Turvy days.

One such day occurred when he was offered an interview at a particular university. He got on the wrong train and ended up in the wrong town. Anyone can make this mistake but it happens so much more often to the dyslexic especially when platform numbers are involved e.g. 6/9, 5/3/2, 3/8; or bus numbers when 69 becomes 96 or 53 becomes 35. The risk is so much greater. Fortunately in Roderick's case he had the sense to catch another train and with the help of a very swift taxi, just made the interview!

NO CONCESSIONS

It was Roderick's wish not to inform the University where he attends that he is dyslexic. He preferred to have no concessions. He coped quite well until the last piece of work before his first year exams when he was accused of "appalling and totally unacceptable spelling" and "Woman's Own" style of writing".

"Generally your laboratory work and effort was quite reasonable — but this report shows much attention needed in this area. A shade too "chatty" and long winded — but the SPELLING! What are you doing about

this? It is quite unacceptable and no mistaking that. Frankly the present standard of spelling and "Woman's Own" chatty style make the reader think the author is a real dreg. — in your professional career you will inevitably be writing for "unknown" readers (e.g. Managing Directors) and the present level MUST be raised all round. Harsh words I realise and not in any way 'personal' — I grieve too!"

Not wanting Roderick to be penalised in an examination for weak spelling, I rang a psychologist acquaintance for advice. He suggested that Roderick should have an up to date assessment and that the College should be informed of the findings so that allowances could be made for the spelling. This has now been done. In the meantime, Roderick spoke to the Head of the Science department who was most sympathetic and understanding.

The things which Roderick has found most difficult during his first year at University are the amount of time it takes to cover all the reading, the difficulty of taking legible and full notes, and the fatigue that results from enormous effort and concentration.

He has met all these problems before however. They are not new to him and he refuses to be defeated by them.

When I started to write this book I asked him when he first realised he was not learning to read as quickly as most of the children in his class, and he gave me two instances immediately. The first was when he was in the infants school and had to go and read to the Headmistress every day. He said "I thought to myself, either she wants to hear me so often because I read nicely and she likes to hear me, or it's because I read so badly that she's going to help me." Then he added "When I looked at the other children who were going with me — I knew it was because I read badly!"

DELIBERATE MISTAKE

The other incident was roughly at the same time. The teacher put a deliberate spelling mistake on the blackboard and then said to the class "When you can spot the mistake come and whisper in my ear and you can go out to play." One by one the class managed to spot it and eventually Roderick was left by himself. "And do you know what Mum?" he said "I couldn't even see the mistake when she showed me." So many times dyslexic children have to miss "play-time" because they are slow, or have to do their work again or have to re-do their spellings. With all the effort most of them make they need their play-time more than most other children who probably do not have to make anywhere near so much effort but end up with much better results.

THE INTERVIEW

In answer to the question "Is there anything which particularly worries you now?" he said that reading aloud was still an ordeal but filling in forms especially in front of people is the worst thing. This is probably because, whilst still at school he went for an interview for a Saturday job loading shelves in a well known chain store. He was handed a four page form to read and fill in on the spot. This almost defeated him. He said he could hardly remember how to spell his own name and naturally he didn't get the job. Given enough time and privacy he can manage perfectly well, and is now getting plenty of practice as he is in the throes of applying for positions when he leaves university.

CHRISTOPHER

Soon after Roderick started Primary School Nigel had begun attending a local play-group for a couple of hours every morning. This left me a great deal of time to spend with my youngest son Christopher who seemed to enjoy every minute of every day. He was always interested in everything around him asking endless questions enquiring about everything he saw, helping in the house, in the garden and with the decorating. He did and still does involve himself in everything, living every minute to the full and gaining experience in many areas.

SPOONERISMS

Christopher was not very happy in his reception class and according to his teacher was not able to remember any "Look and Say" words for reading. She said to me "I tell him over and over again what they are but he still doesn't know. He can't even remember them from one minute to the next." This didn't sound like Christopher who had always grasped everything so quickly at home. He was the one of my children with astonishingly sound common sense — a reliable down to earth lad who was always asking sensible questions and making good conversation. He did make spoonerisms it's true, but so do lots of other children of five years old. He used to say:-

"Beg and acorn" for "egg and bacon"
"Spark and Markers" for "Marks and Spencers"
"Par Cark" for "Car Park"
"Teg on Oast" for "Egg on Toast"

"WHAT PREVENTS HIM FROM LEARNING?"

However, as the teacher was rather concerned we had a discussion. In view of the fact that Christopher appeared to be bright enough what was it that was preventing him from learning? We went through all the things it could be.

He had no physical defects apart from a very slight lisp. He had had the usual medical examination when he started school and eyes and ears were functioning adequately. (I was interested to notice however, that the eye test using the capital E was no longer being used.)

There was no apparent emotional disturbance, he came from a stimulating environment and there had been no long period of separation from the family. Any one of these things can cause reading retardation.

The teacher then showed me some of his work — certainly he found great difficulty copying from the blackboard or even from a book and the writing was poor. All the ball and stick letters b p d g q were being confused and in his newsbook every time he had drawn our house it had the number 65 on the door even though we lived at 56.

HEREDITY?
I made no mention of my thoughts to this most caring teacher but to myself I said "Oh not again!" Christopher was making all the same mistakes that Roderick did. Why should this be? Did this disability run in families? I decided to keep a careful eye on the situation and continued to note the types of mistakes he made and the sort of things he said and did.

At about this same time in the class I was teaching there was a group of children who needed more help than the rest of the class. Two of them were from broken homes with traumatic histories, one had very poor eyesight, two were slow learners (i.e. children who are intellectually slow and take longer to learn everything) and one was a puzzle to me. Little by little, slowly but surely the first five were beginning to learn in spite of their difficulties but the sixth one who seemed to have everything he needed, wasn't making any headway at all. He came from a good secure home with caring parents. He had a lively personality and made good conversation. He seemed bright enough but his reading was almost non-existent and his written work was strange with peculiar spidery writing and letters and words all jumbled up. He made the most bizarre efforts at copying and yet he tried so hard all the time.

This boy was right handed but one day broke his right arm in an accident and returned to school with the arm in plaster. I was not expecting him to do any written work for several weeks but instead he simply picked up the pencil with his left hand and wrote. The writing seemed better than usual. My first thought was that this poor boy had been made to use his right hand for writing when he was really left handed and that was the possible cause of his difficulties and slowness in acquiring written language skills. As soon as the plaster was removed however, he returned to writing with his right hand so it was obviously the one he preferred. Over the weeks I made very little headway with this splendid lad who never gave up trying.

NO RETENTION

As was the custom in the school all the slow readers were helped by the Head teacher who gave them individual tuition and eventually the lad began to read but it was a slow and exhausting business for both student and teacher. His mother was naturally concerned about him and spoke to me when she visited the school. I had to admit I was perplexed by him. Although he had now made a start with reading, I was unable to teach him to spell accurately and his written work was still poor. He could not retain words for even a short time to write them down and he reversed letters and words and continued to spell in a most bizarre way. Looking back I feel that this boy was the first dyslexic child I had tried to teach but whatever I tried to do didn't seem to help him. I tried everything I knew, particularly learning through his interests but to no avail.

DYSLEXIA — NOT SO RARE AFTER ALL

It crossed my mind several times how like Roderick he was — perhaps this dyslexia wasn't such a rare thing after all. I certainly didn't mention my feelings to anyone — after all Roderick seemed to be getting on fairly well — perhaps this boy would too. In those days even though I was a teacher I knew nothing about referring a child to the London hospitals for assessment and diagnosis and that, in fact, it might be possible to teach these children so that they would learn. This was in the very early days when Dyslexia Societies were just being formed but I was unaware of them. I learned several years later that his parents had in fact become members of a Dyslexia Society and had received help in getting the boy referred. He then attended The Word Blind Centre in London and later went to a boarding school where the teachers knew how to teach dyslexics and he had done very well. For my part I know he was my first real failure.

The second came the following year — another boy with a similar story, another boy whom I was failing. This problem was obviously not uncommon but what was the answer? At this time I simply did not know, and yet I was a trained and caring teacher with experience and felt I *should* have known.

SYSTEMATIC TEACHING

I was to meet this second boy again years later when he was in secondary school. He had had remedial help all through his school life with little result. When I finally caught up with him he was being taught by a psychologist who was at that time teaching in a Remedial Unit. She was using such a splendid systematic way of teaching that the boy was at last beginning to achieve. The reason I saw her teaching was through my youngest son Christopher.

To recap a little in the story, Christopher had had three years in the infant school and in that time learned and experienced many things. The skills he did not acquire however, were reading, writing and spelling. Each teacher in turn had worked very hard with him and he tried very hard in return — always willing to have another go. When the effort finally became too great he appeared to "switch off". As one teacher said, "When he pulls the curtain across, I know that's it. It's no good going on."

HATED THE TEACHER

Even though he was still poor at the language skills by the time he entered junior school I didn't feel too worried. The other two sons seemed to be coping fairly well and Christopher would undoubtedly be the same. Once again we would wait and see what happened. All went well for a little while and then he started to be very unhappy telling me he hated the teacher and wanted to kill her. He began asking me why he was so stupid. Constant reassurances were no good. Apparently his teacher continued to tell him he was stupid so he insisted that stupid he must be. Whatever had happened to change my happy youngest son into this angry and frustrated boy! It appeared he was finding the work very hard and was having to stay in at play-times. He also had to go to remedial reading classes with a group of boys whom he had always regarded as disruptive and he hated it. I was meeting children in the street who delighted in telling me that Christopher had been sent out of the classroom over and over again, and had been threatened with being sent back to the infants school if his reading didn't improve. It was obvious he was beginning to become a thorough nuisance so I decided it was best to sort things out before they became worse. I made an appointment to see the Headmaster, a splendid man, who really liked his job and children, and always did his utmost to help.

SURPRISED

He listened to my story and decided that at my insistence, it would be a good idea if Christopher was assessed at the Child Guidance Clinic to determine exactly what was the cause of the trouble. I confided to the Headteacher that I really felt Christopher to be dyslexic and should this be so, he would need specialist teaching, but where he was to get it I didn't know. I was rather surprised that the Head didn't know what dyslexia was, and yet I don't know why I should have felt surprised. I had only recently started reading about it myself, and until a few months earlier I had never heard of it either.

In due course we were given an appointment at the Child Guidance Clinic. Christopher was taken into the psychologist's room and as it apparently wasn't going to be a long session I waited in the waiting room reading magazines and thinking "Splendid, I'm sure our problems are about to be resolved." I should soon know all the answers. After what seemed to be a very short while, the psychologist brought Christopher out and told me that he was an averagely intelligent boy who had a reading problem. This he had decided was manifesting itself in bad behaviour! Is this what I had come for? He was only telling me what I had told the Headmaster. I wanted to know *why* Chris had a reading problem and what we were going to do to help him. The psychologist seemed to ignore the first part of the question, but answered the second part by telling me of the availability of the Remedial Centre, and for the 'behaviour' problem, the Child Guidance Clinic. I already knew of both these services but remember saying "I think Christopher has a specific difficulty (not mentioning the word dyslexia) and I feel he should be taught by someone who understands this, and knows how to cope with it". This didn't stir him to comment and in my innocence I left thinking I should be receiving a written copy of the findings. This of course did not happen, although I understand now that parents

who *ask*, do receive something in writing.
ANGRY
A few days later I received a telephone call from the
Headmaster of the school saying that he had received a
copy of the report and if I would like to discuss it with
him I could do so. A mutual date was arranged and I
arrived saying that I hadn't yet received my report. It was
only at that stage I learned I wasn't going to get one. He
explained that parents were not given anything in
writing. I felt somewhat annoyed, cheated, even peeved
at this, and suggested that I could perhaps read his
copy. I couldn't believe my ears when he apologised
profusely and said that it was confidential and on no
account was I to see it. Here was I, the caring parent
who had specifically asked for help for her child with
difficulties, only to be told that I couldn't see the
findings. I can only assume that the report indicated that
the "over-anxious mother" was the *cause* of the
problems. I felt furious and the poor Headteacher was
obviously very embarrassed at my anger. Although very
angry, I felt that if that was the "rule" I must abide by it,
but I often wish now that I had made more fuss and
demanded to see the psychologist again. However, in
retrospect, this may not have been wise. I should only
have been labelled "neurotic" "excitable" "over
anxious" and probably been offered therapy for my
condition!

Returning to the interview, I felt I must not let my anger
get in the way of helping Christopher so when the Head
asked me if I wanted Christopher to go to the Remedial
Centre my answer was "Yes, but only on condition there
is a teacher there who understands dyslexic children and
knows how to teach them." If Chris was of average

intelligence he was quite capable of learning to read and spell providing the teaching was geared to his needs. If he couldn't learn on the "Look and Say" method, and he couldn't learn on the "phonic" method, he would have to be taught some other way. The teacher I was looking for must know the "other" way whatever it was and unlock the code for Christopher. I had read enough by this time to know that ordinary remedial teaching was not going to work.

The poor Headmaster wanting only to do his best for Christopher, could not say whether my demands were possible but suggested that I "give it a try". He said he would arrange it.

SPECIALIST TEACHING
Very shortly afterwards, I received a letter from the Headmistress of the local Remedial Unit giving me a date to go and meet her and discuss Christopher. My husband and I went together. Sometimes at the last moment I seem to lack the courage of my convictions but my husband is always there, supporting, helping and encouraging. I was armed with my little booklet on Dyslexia from Aston University and "Diagnosis in the Classroom" by Gill Cotterill and I must say I was prepared for a tussle should it arise. Considering the emotional connotations that the word dyslexia had at that time, the Head was extremely diplomatic, and after listening to my story said that she had a member of staff who knew about dyslexia and had been on a course specialising in the teaching of dyslexics. I was delighted at this and she suggested that my husband and I should meet her. We were shown into a little room and there was the boy I had failed all those years before. He was being taught by this psychologist-teacher and he was

actually learning. I was fascinated and couldn't wait for Christopher to get started. This he did the following week.

LEARNING WAS NOW EXCITING
I find it difficult to explain the change that came over him. At last Christopher had found someone who really seemed to understand him and speak his language — someone who was really on the same wavelength and was teaching him in a manner in which he was able to learn. His joy was beyond belief. He returned to being a happy boy and learning was now exciting. He could even shrug off the comments of his peers as he left for his lesson. "Going to the daft school again?" "Botley" "Spastic". These remarks hurt I know, but Chris felt it was worth all the hurt, now that he was learning so much more easily.

After a few sessions the teacher invited me with Christopher's agreement, to sit in on one of the lessons. I was very impressed by what I saw, a properly structured method of teaching with the child learning in a multi-sensory way, i.e. learning through all his senses simultaneously.

I asked Christopher's remedial teacher where she had acquired her knowledge of this method and the structure she was using which included spelling choices, spelling rules, etc. She told me the name of a person who has since become not only my tutor, and guide, but also a very dear friend. This person was almost due to retire from her position as Head of a Remedial Centre. Apparently she was to give a lecture locally about her six month visit to America where she had been studying at the Scottish Rite hospital in Dallas. The lecture was to be accompanied by slides and a film. That lecture was a revelation.

JOY OF SUCCESS

I have rarely experienced such a stimulating couple of hours in my career as a teacher. After the meeting I asked if the speaker ran courses and I signed on for the last one before she retired. That course really opened my eyes to the problems of the dyslexic in the classroom and taught me how to begin making his life easier and subsequently how to teach him so that he would feel this joy of success.

Some professionals who do not acknowledge dyslexia put the child's difficulties down to bad teaching. There may be isolated cases where a child has been unfortunate enough not to learn because of a bad teacher but in my experience this is rare. Some children seem to learn in any situation and with any teacher. I believe that most teachers are caring people but they are human. They can't know everything, no one is perfect and there are only so many hours in the day. If by bad teaching the critics mean that the teaching has not been geared to the specific needs of the child concerned, then I would agree that this is the reason the child has not learnt. It is easy to blame the poor class teacher for this but teaching the dyslexic is not always easy in a class of 36 or more.

MULTI-SENSORY TEACHING

I have since learned and firmly believe, that if all children were taught in a multi-sensory way when they started school, the "Look and Say" learners wouldn't suffer, the "phonic" learners wouldn't suffer and the dyslexic child would have a chance to learn along with everyone else instead of experiencing failure which often leads to emotional disturbance and further difficulties.

Whilst attending the course I was putting some of my new found knowledge into practice with my class. I was finding however, that I was spending more and more time with the 'slow group' and getting very excited by their progress. I was wishing I could concentrate on this group all the time but there were other things to do, maths, games, art, craft and many other children to teach in my busy classroom.

As luck would have it a part time vacancy occurred at the local Remedial Unit for which I applied and was successful. I started to work there but for only two days each week. This was the first time I was able to put my new-found knowledge into operation all day long together with experience I had acquired throughout my teaching life.

SLOW PROGRESS
Christopher was attending lessons at the Remedial Unit twice a week but his days and mine did not coincide. He was really beginning to read now and enjoy it. Progress was slow and sometimes painful but he was succeeding. His spelling was still very weak but he persevered and began to apply some of his spelling choices and rules. He began to settle down at school but found it hard to forgive his class teacher for her lack of understanding and was relieved when he reached his second year and a new teacher. Apart from the odd unhappy incident, he began to enjoy school again. The tuition at the Remedial Unit was giving him back his

confidence and he was beginning to cope slowly. Unfortunately he hadn't Roderick's ability in maths but he was better at sport and very good at craft, especially woodwork. On the whole the teachers tried to understand his difficulties but basically they considered it a reading problem only, and expected that now he was beginning to read he should be able to spell.

SPELLING "AS IT SOUNDS"

I too used to think that, but for someone who cannot recall words accurately because of poor visual ability, spelling remains very difficult. If a person cannot rely on visually recalling a word, he usually tries to spell it by sound. If his sequencing is good, he may get the sounds in the correct order, and luckily if a word is spelt as it sounds, it will be correct. If the word is a sight word or an irregular word e.g. 'said' — this will be written "sed", 'once' will be written "wuns", 'use' will be written "yooz". So often children are given lists of spellings to learn. They copy them from the board, take them home to learn them, and then they are tested on them a few days later. This was certainly true in Christopher's case. For some children this is not a bad thing and some do learn this way, but the dyslexic child will probably copy his list down inaccurately to start with, and take it home incomplete. He tries to learn words and may manage one or two but for how long will he retain that learning? A day, or two days? A week? He may manage to get one or two correct in the test providing they are given in the same order but if the teacher jumbles the order he's in real trouble.

These spelling lists often contain words such as:-

bought	when
bough	where
brought	why
through	who
though	whom
thought	whose
cough	what

Many of these words look so alike the dyslexic becomes confused and finds them very troublesome.
Unfortunately, he may have made a desperate effort to learn them but the results do not reflect this effort.

FAMILIES OF WORDS
It is much kinder to give a dyslexic families of words to learn, for example:-

igh	ing
fight	sing
night	thing
light	bringing
sight	swinging
high	sting
	cling

These he may well be able to cope with.

Christopher's reports were on the whole, encouraging. It was certainly recognised that he had a problem even if the reasons and the implication of it weren't understood. The remarks in his reports now contained comments on his improvement in reading and his diligence and perseverance in attitude. Spelling continued to be difficult however, and gave rise to such remarks as:-

"Spelling still wildly inaccurate"

"Spelling still a weak point"

"Spelling still needs a great deal of concentrated effort"

"You must try harder with your spelling"

DEVELOPMENTAL DYSLEXIA

One day after his lesson at the Remedial Unit, the teacher suggested to me that it would be a good idea for Christopher to have a private assessment as up to now it was only my feeling and hers that Christopher was dyslexic. I rang the National Hospital and made an appointment for both Roderick and Christopher to be assessed by Dr Macdonald Critchley, a well known British Neurologist. After seeing both boys individually for a considerable time, he spoke at length to my husband and myself. He informed us that the boys were indeed the victims of developmental dyslexia. He felt that Roderick was now performing fairly well and had on the whole, overcome his difficulties, but Christopher would continue to need a great deal of help. Before leaving, he explained that it might be necessary for the boys to have certificates to enable them to obtain concessions in examinations, and he would be willing to issue these when necessary. We were most grateful. This was the first time we had known this was even possible.

DESTRUCTIVE COMMENTS

At one point during Christopher's secondary school life, he had been going through a rather tough time working very hard but repeatedly having destructive comments on every piece of work. Eventually I wrote a letter which was published in the Dyslexia Review. It reads:-

"As the parent of a dyslexic child I am incensed as all

such parents are when I read discouraging and often unjust remarks which some teachers write on my child's efforts. As a teacher I am appalled at the thoughtlessness these teachers show in making such remarks and the evident lack of training given which would enable them to recognise the signs of dyslexia.

Here are some examples taken from recent exercises in my fourteen year old son's books!

"You take very little care to do your work properly"
"You haven't copied it correctly"
"You must be careful when you copy the questions down"
"A good idea for a story Christopher but you obviously did not read your work through! Now corrections please"
"Interesting Chris, but what are we going to do about your spelling and punctuation?"
"You must get to grips with your reading, Chris. Always choose a book you **can** read".

I know that other parents have many similar examples. What makes the matter even more aggravating and frustrating is that the school may have been repeatedly informed of the problem and the various ways in which it can manifest itself. In spite of these repeated efforts on my part, some teachers, particularly those new to the staff, are evidently not informed and fail to perceive the signs of dyslexia. The most frequent offenders seem to be teachers of English and other languages. Obviously they have found written language so easy it is impossible for them to comprehend the difficulties of this boy. These are the lucky people who, one assumes, must have reliable auditory and visual perception, good *sequential ability and memory span. No doubt it does seem odd to such teachers that one minute my son can spell a word correctly and the next minute he cannot; that sometimes he can spell a word verbally then writes it down wrongly; that he makes transpositions and omissions, reverses his letters from time to time and misses out syllables; that he copies inaccurately from the blackboard and puts upper case B's and D's everywhere because he cannot be certain which way round they face in lower case.*

Maybe the training colleges are partly to blame for the apparent ignorance of the teachers who often show such lack of understanding. Perhaps if they had been instructed in college how to look into a child's work and analyse his errors and if they had studied language structure and how to teach it they would be able to offer constructive instead of destructive criticisms.

The teachers themselves however must take some of the responsibility. If a child is continually making mistakes a teacher must be prepared to ask himself several questions. "Why is this boy failing?" "What am I not doing for him that I should be doing?" "How can I help him?" "Is there something which I do not understand and about which I must discover more?"

I know there are many teachers who have asked themselves these questions and are seeking the answers but obviously there are still many who are not aware that such a problem even exists.

Of course there would be no problem if the dyslexic child could be diagnosed earlier in a clinic such as the one run by Dr Curtis Jenkins* and could have the benefit of a planned programme of suitable activities to be

*A local General Practitioner with a personal interest in Dyslexia.

carried out either at home or in the nursery school. This could then lead on to a properly structured language programme with multi-sensory learning such as that which is carried out at the Dyslexia Institute.

The teaching of dyslexic children should not have to be considered remedial work. Detected early enough and given the right type of teaching in their schools from the beginning these children would not have to experience failure and frustration.

All teachers in training should be taught what to look for in a dyslexic child and if the training colleges cannot find the time in their curriculum to accommodate lectures on the subject they should certainly be prepared to inform their students where to go to acquire further training.

However, until such a happy state of affairs arrives, dyslexic children will no doubt continue to suffer the unhelpful type of comments listed above: comments which are likely to turn the most conscientious child into an unhappy and disheartened adolescent."

I later discovered that this letter had been re-printed in an Australian Dyslexia Magazine which in turn had been sent to a psychologist I know working in a language disability clinic in Montreal. She wrote to tell me that she had pinned it up in the waiting room of her clinic where it could be read by all the parents. It seems that problems are similar all over the world.

A TOTAL LANGUAGE PROBLEM
In fact just before this letter was published in the Dyslexia Review, I was invited to my son's school, to speak on the subject of Dyslexia and I have always been most grateful for this opportunity. The staff were

tremendously kind and listened with great interest, asking many questions and realising for the first time that in fact dyslexia is a total language problem with many inexplicable factors which account for lots of other difficulties like directional and sequencing problems.

Certainly Christopher met with a great deal of understanding afterwards. The only time he has had really unthoughtful comments on his work is when a new teacher or a student joins the staff who hasn't been informed of the situation. This happened fairly recently when a student teacher wrote the following:-

"This work is spoilt by stupid spelling errors."
If this young man had known Christopher's history and how hard he works to overcome his problem it is unlikely that he would have written the word 'stupid'. I looked through the piece of work. There were few mistakes that I could see:

> peaces for pieces
> beach for beech
> oppersite for opposite
> parrellel for parallel

To the layman I suppose they do look like careless errors but are they? I think not. I would consider them to be intelligent attempts and commendable efforts. I do not feel angry with this teacher but I do feel sad. I remember all too well the days when I thought the same as he. I hope he won't take as long to learn as I did.

Christopher is now beginning his O level year. He will take O levels in the subjects for which he shows most aptitude and C.S.E. in the others. It seems unlikely at this stage he will get a C.S.E. grade 1 in English which is the only grade equivalent to an English O level. Fortunately, however, he does not need English O level for his chosen career. It has been his ambition for some time now to become a stage manager or lighting technician and he has had an interview and been accepted for a Theatre School where he can study these courses.

PERSEVERANCE — AND PARENTAL SUPPORT
Christopher will begin his training in the autumn of his seventeenth year. It seems to be an ideal career for him. He has always been a practical down to earth boy with his feet firmly planted on the ground. He knows where he is going and he will get there. He has the perseverance and dedication necessary, and he knows what hard work is. He has always had to work extremely hard and that, together with the support he has always had from home, has built his character strengths. He is also blessed with enormous reserves of energy.

Parental support is so necessary. It is important for a child who perhaps has had a frustrating, often harrowing day, to be able to come home and talk and feel that home is a place where people don't consider him stupid or lazy. A place where he can unwind with people he knows will support and encourage him.

NIGEL

At this stage the reader may well ask "What about Nigel?" I confess that I have deliberately left until last talking about my second son. For Nigel has had similar experiences to the other boys but he is different. He is a constant reminder to me that however long one has been teaching, no matter how well qualified one is, however experienced we are as parents or teachers, we simply never know it all. As in most walks of life, the more we learn the more we realise how much more there is still to learn.

Nigel was never an easy baby like the other two who seemed to eat and sleep at sociable hours. He was a difficult baby who cried a great deal. He seemed not to be interested in food and slept very little. He would never have a long afternoon nap like the others — he just didn't seem to need sleep. Evenings were often the worst — it was then he would start being really lively, jumping up and down and laughing. As soon as he was put into his cot however he would start the crying which eventually turned to screaming. Night after night he was awake for hours while we, his parents, were getting more and more exhausted. The doctor was fairly unhelpful. "There's nothing physically wrong with him — he's bloody minded — some babies are — leave him alone a bit more — he'll get over it."

Well, I didn't know a great deal about babies apart from my own but I couldn't think a baby cries for *nothing* and I didn't think the doctor's advice very helpful. Anyway there is a limit to how long you can listen to your baby in distress and to how much tolerance the neighbours have. In retrospect if I had thought to play records to him until he slept it might have helped but at that time I had no way of knowing how much he would grow to love music and how many hours he would spend listening to it.

UNSTABLE IMAGES?

The situation improved over the months but still he suffered from extreme bouts of crying which seemed to have no explanation. Even when he was cuddled the crying did not stop. Was he experiencing unstable images I wonder, where he was not recognising things which should have been familiar and so was afraid? I do not know for sure of course but in the light of further experience I feel this may have been the reason for some of his distress.

He was an exasperating toddler in many ways, quick moving and always seeming to cause havoc by knocking piles of cans down in supermarkets and having moods which changed almost like magic from laughter to tears and vice versa in a split second. Just at the moment when I felt I couldn't take any more he would look at me with his big blue eyes, smile, run into my arms and smother me with kisses. He has always had a lot of energy. At eighteen he still does not require much sleep and is often at his best between 11p.m. and 2 or 3 o'clock in the morning. He may go to bed between 11-12 but is often listening to music two hours later.

UNCONVENTIONAL

I have never been able to understand the way he thinks — he certainly never approaches anything from a conventional angle and this is confirmed by the man for whom he works who says that Nigel always "gets there in the end but what a roundabout route he takes." He simply doesn't seem to use the same channels as everyone else. Is this the reason why he sometimes seems to be out of step with the world?

Nigel had four terms at the play group before starting school. He thoroughly enjoyed it and so looked forward to going to "proper school". There he was happy from the beginning. Many of his play group friends were in the same class. He was popular with both his peers and with adults — he made friends easily. Nigel was good at sport; he had a talent for mimicry; he liked dressing up and acting; he joined in all school activities one hundred per cent.

'LEARNING BY DOING'

He had joined a local dancing school where he attended every Saturday morning. Together with sport, dancing was one of his chief passions in life and he took to it well. Learning a sequence of steps appeared to be no problem because he moved through the sequence as he learned it rather than by being 'talked at'. 'Learning by doing' has always been easier for Nigel. It is true that at this time Nigel showed little interest in matters more academic, but his teachers spoke well of him.

Certainly his reports commented on his weak spelling and lack of concentration. On the other hand they praised him highly in the areas where he was succeeding. It was suggested to me that when he went to secondary school he would knuckle down and make much more effort. Once his efforts were rewarded with success he would be fine.

BORED AND DISRUPTIVE

Nigel's secondary school years however, were not happy and he often said how bored he was. He consequently "fooled around" and was often in trouble. At the end of his second year the comments from his teachers were disturbing. He was doing very little work and was often disruptive. It seemed that all the things *he* was interested in, the school was not, and he was not interested in anything that went on at school. He even stopped working at sport and drama. Eventually after discussion with him it was decided that an assessment be arranged for him. This was done. The assessment found him to be a boy of good average intellectual ability but with the same dyslexic tendencies as the other boys. Unfortunately, if you are dyslexic you must work twice as hard as normal to succeed and if you are not motivated to work hard, academic success is not for you. Some people of course mature much later than others and often decide to study later in life.

LEARNING A TRADE

Nigel however, as I have already said, is a 'learner by doing' and although he had little academic success at school was lucky enough to be taken on as an apprentice with a car-engineering firm where he is doing very well. He seems happier now than he has been for the last five years. He is learning a trade. If ever he feels the need to extend his education he will be able to do so. There are many opportunities for later study now.

Which brings me back to what I said at the beginning of this chapter. I hope that in the end Nigel will be able to find his own particular niche in life and be happy in it, whether it be as a car mechanic, or playing the drums which he does with zest, or doing something altogether different. Nevertheless I still feel that it is a pity that neither I nor his school seemed able to help him during those earlier years. I am still not sure to what extent the dyslexic tendencies which Nigel undoubtedly shares with his brothers went unrecognised and thereby contributed to his lack of achievement at school.

FAMILY INTERESTS

I think it is not fully understood how dyslexia affects many aspects of daily life, for example hobbies. These may have to be restricted. In our particular case our family hobby is the amateur stage and all three sons show great interest and some aptitude for both acting and back-stage work. The difficulty with acting however, is that it is a great advantage to be an efficient sight reader if you wish to audition for a part in a play. In school plays it is extremely rare for a poor reader to get a good acting part because if he auditions badly, it is assumed he would not be able to act the part. Good readers usually get good parts.

Luckily, the family all belong to a drama society which has a very flourishing youth section and the boys have gained experience in all areas of dramatic and musical theatre in spite of being hesitant readers when required to read out loud in front of other people. It is often possible to get hold of a script a week or so before auditions and prepare a passage. This helps a great deal. All boys have enough confidence now to attend drama courses organised at various colleges, including the Bristol Old Vic, which have widened their experience.

DRAWBACKS
Working back-stage of course can have its drawbacks as was discovered when the junior players were entering an Alan Ayckbourn play in a drama festival. Christopher was allocated the job of making two notices for a library

scene. They had to be big notices and he worked solidly one Sunday measuring the materials, printing and painting, and then proudly presented his two works of art.

These were they:-

Fortunately, a sheet of sticky paper and a little more time soon made them acceptable.

IN THE CHOIR

An activity which came to a somewhat untimely end was singing in the Church Choir. This appealed very much to Christopher.

I rather think it was the payment for weddings which was the main attraction but nevertheless he was keen to join the choir. Unfortunately, the chief choir boy was a clever lad who certainly had no difficulties. He was a most efficient reader and beautiful singer but totally lacked patience with anyone who couldn't match his standards. Being a new boy Christopher had to stand next to the chief choir boy whom I hoped was there to help him. This help however, consisted of Chris being elbowed in the ribs every time he stopped singing, the simple reason being that he couldn't read the words. He was black and blue after a few weeks and even the thought of the wedding money would not persuade him to continue. He has recently taken up bell ringing however. It isn't particularly easy for him because it

involves sequencing. Roderick could never get the hang of it, and continually in practices, fouled up the peal. The team of campanologists were very tolerant but in the end he was asked politely to "give it up".
Christopher however, up to now, is having a little more success at it, and appears to be enjoying the experience greatly.

AVOID SCRABBLE!
Some social occasions are not always enjoyable experiences particularly if word games are involved. Treasure hunts are fun but only if you can read the clues. Scrabble is a game to be avoided at all costs. It is so sad that someone who can't spell is either a huge joke, or considered dumb. Dyslexics understandably avoid putting themselves in this type of situation, and one cannot blame them.

Telling the time has always been a fairly hazardous business. I recall one day when I asked Roderick, then about nine years old, what was the time. There was silence for a second or two while he studied his watch and then he said, "Well, it's either quarter to or quarter past." A conventional watch was unreliable for Roderick, so as soon as possible he had a digital one. This we thought would solve the problem with before and after. I should have known this solution was a little too simple. If you see numbers the wrong way round 12.32 can easily be read as 21.23 unless you are looking very carefully and concentrating very hard. Over the years however, his ability to tell the time has undoubtedly improved although he still misreads a conventional clock and often sets his alarm clock at the wrong time.

"WHAT SIDE DO THE PLATES GO?"

Laying the table is also a risky business although I feel
this is probably due mainly to the fact that Roderick is
left handed. I am repeatedly asked "Which side do the
plates go?" When I answer "the left hand side" I am
never surprised to see them on the right and the knives
and forks on the opposite side to where they should be.
No day is dull in our house — one never knows quite
what to expect or where to expect it.

GETTING THE MESSAGE

Taking telephone messages was not without its
complications. If a written message was involved, it was
usually written in an almost code-like spelling which was
impossible to decipher. After ages trying, I would
suggest to the son who had written it "Would you like
to read the message to me?" This usually resulted in the
reply "I don't know what it says, I can't read it and I
can't remember the message". If asked immediately
after writing something in bizarre spelling a dyslexic will
sometimes be able to remember what he's written but
after a gap of minutes, hours, days, weeks, he will have
no idea what it says. This type of difficulty of course
creates grave problems for revision when the notes
which are being used to revise from, were taken at
speed and are often inaccurate and incomplete.

Returning to the phone messages, it was explained to
the boys that rather than attempt to take a message,
they should simply take the number of the caller
explaining that mother or father were busy but would
ring back later. This worked a little better but of course
those readers who know dyslexics' problems will realise
that taking down a five, six or seven digit number in the
correct order is nearly as bad as taking down the

message, and I think for some adults it is even worse. There certainly were many times when I had to say "I'm sorry to have troubled you" after I had dialled the number the boys had given me. Instead of 52283 they had written down 25283 or 22538 or any combination of the digits. They are all certainly much better now and there is hardly ever a mistake because they are so careful. The only funny incident recently was the message on the pad, "Uncle Brain phoned!" instead of "Uncle Brian phoned"

Like many other families, we often enjoy an evening's television. Some time ago, I took part in a television documentary myself on the subject of dyslexia called "If you knew Susie". It was some time before the film was edited and shown on television but finally the evening arrived and the family all settled down to watch. There were few comments while it was on, but at the end of the programme the captions started rolling and Christopher spoke, "Well", said he, "Thank goodness I had help early — at least I'm over all that reversal business" and then "What's a budding mixer?" "Dubbing mixers" will always be known as "Budding mixers" in our house from now on. What a postscript to a programme on dyslexia!

While on a shopping expedition one day he looked at a notice which said PRAM RAMP. "Why have they written that word twice?" he asked.

Words flashed up on the television screen are often misunderstood by the dyslexic. A similar incident crosses my mind which happened to a twelve year old boy whom I teach. He was writing about motor bikes but couldn't think how to spell goggles. After a while he asked me and then said "Oh no, wait a minute, I remember seeing that word on a television advert." He closed his eyes trying to recall the image of the word, said "Got it" and promptly wrote "doddles".

Roderick's main hobby for several years was bicycle building. He used to buy up really dilapidated old bikes or search through scrap yards for any parts which could be salvaged. He then renovated these parts and built new bikes out of old ones. At first he would advertise a finished bike for sale but before long people were ringing up, placing orders! He built up a very lucrative little business. Now of course he is too busy to continue but does manage to keep his little mini in tip top condition.

Knowing his history of directional difficulties people often ask me if I worry about Roderick driving. The answer is, yes I do worry about it especially as he once had a very nasty accident on his bike. I just pray he will not attempt to drive when he is overtired and as he has always had to do with reading and writing, remembers to *look* and *think* very carefully.

FOR PARENTS

At this point I should like to say that from here on I shall use the pronoun 'he' when referring to the dyslexic child. Not only is this less clumsy than saying "he or she" each time but in my experience a larger number of boys than girls suffer from these difficulties, probably about five to one. It must be understood however that everything I say applies as much to girls as to boys.

To parents I would like to say this.

You must support your child every step of the way. You know him better than anyone else. You will be the first to know if he is unhappy at school and you must be prepared to try and find out what is wrong. It is up to you to approach the school and speak to his teacher even if you do get labelled "over anxious". In my experience parents are not anxious unless they have something to be anxious about, and the unhappiness of their children is bound to cause anxiety.

Your child may be lucky enough to have a teacher who is already aware of the situation and finds it puzzling. The teacher may then ask you to visit the school for a discussion. If this happens, your child is in the most caring hands.

ASSESSING INTELLECTUAL ABILITY

If the situation does not improve it is advisable to ask the Headteacher of your child's school to arrange an assessment with an educational psychologist. Not all psychologists like the term "dyslexia" but that is not really so important. A psychologist will be able to assess your child's intellectual ability and determine what the specific problems are. He should then advise on the type of help necessary.

If you are still not satisfied you could approach one of
the London Hospitals (addresses at the end of the
book) for a further assessment on the National Health.
This is often arranged through your family practitioner.
This may take quite a time due to the demand. If this is
so, and money is no obstacle it is a good idea to
arrange for a private assessment in which case the
parent is normally given a full and comprehensive report
of the findings plus suggestions for the remediation.
Remember a diagnosis in itself is pointless — it is the
correct treatment i.e. the appropriate teaching method
which is the important factor.

TRY TO BE CALM
It is inadvisable to approach the school in an angry or
aggressive manner though you may feel like it. It rarely
serves any useful purpose and often aggravates an
already emotional situation. Try to be calm and don't
think the teacher is uncaring. She has many other
children to teach and may well be giving your child a
great deal of extra time already. If an assessment has
been carried out and your child referred to a dyslexic
clinic or a remedial centre, the teacher in charge of the
programme of learning is the best adviser of how you
can assist at home.

Note the remarks in his school report carefully. They
may be comments like:-

- Must try harder
- Lazy
- Careless
- Oral work good, written work poor
- Must work harder at spelling
- Must read more
- Exam result disappointing

VALUE OF PRAISE

Certainly always praise your child for the things he can do well instead of commenting on his weaknesses. Your child may have many practical aptitudes and these should be encouraged. I have known several dyslexic boys who are most proficient at assembling new bicycles out of old ones and make quite a bit of pocket money this way. Many are also very clever at making models and building with Meccano and Lego — these boys and girls are the engineers of the future. I know a dyslexic girl who has just finished her first year as an engineering student and is doing very well.

Erase the words "lazy" "slow" "stupid" from your vocabulary. You know he isn't any of these things but he will inevitably be called so. Clumsy he may well be. Do try to be patient about this. He cannot help knocking things over, and drawing attention to it will only make the situation worse. If you know your child has these tendencies don't have expensive antiques around. It is only asking for trouble and will make you and him very nervous.

Be patient with coat fastening and shoe lace tying. Don't do these things for him even though it will be much quicker if you do. He has to learn to do them by himself and mustn't be rushed. In the meantime, perhaps slip-on or even buckle shoes, are the answer and a tie on an elastic is useful for a small child. When helping him to tie a proper tie don't suggest he looks in a mirror — this will only add to the confusion. Stand behind him and help him from behind.

READ TO YOUR CHILD

Continue to read to him. He will probably need it much longer than other children. Even when he starts reading it won't be easy for him and he will soon tire. He needs to be read to — nursery rhymes, stories, poetry, and factual books, so that he will not fall behind with his vocabulary and information. If he misses out on these early words because he cannot read them for himself, his language could well remain deprived.

When you are reading to him, let him sit beside you with him holding the book so that he can follow the words as you read. It will help him if you move your finger along under the words as you read so that he associates the *look* of the word with the *sound* of the word and he gets practice moving his eyes from left to right across the page. It is often expected that children automatically move their eyes efficiently from left to right when reading but the dyslexic does not. He may well have erratic eye movements and often lose his place. When he is reading himself, a window marker may be useful so that he can see only the line he is reading. (See diagram).

USE A TAPE RECORDER

You may have to help with reading well into the secondary school especially if your child is required to read a book every six weeks or so to write a review on it. Because he will read slowly, you may have to be prepared to read every other chapter to him. If this is not acceptable to him suggest you, the parents, read the chapter into the tape recorder and then he can listen to it on his own, following the script as he listens.

I would like to devote a few lines here to recording material. First of all choose your material carefully. For young children I recommend the Lady Bird information books and the Lady Bird Fairy Tale books. They are clearly written, beautifully illustrated and ideal for this purpose.

It is essential to read in a clear, slow but interesting voice and give the instructions at the beginning of the tape. I have made many of these tapes which have been most useful. It is a good idea to label the tapes clearly for obvious reasons and keep them with the books.

RECORDING TIPS

Make sure the child knows which is the *beginning* of the book and can find the page where the story begins.

This is how I begin my tapes.

This is story of 'Cinderella' (or whatever the story happens to be.)

I am going to read it to you and I want you to follow the words as I read them.

At the end of each page you will hear this sound (little bell). When you hear it I want you to turn the page over.

If you wish to look at the picture switch off the machine and switch on again when you are ready. We are now ready to begin.

Repetition is marvellous for children and they will listen to the same stories over and over again. It is very useful to build up a little library of taped stories and teach your child how to use the tape recorder so that when you are busy he is beneficially and enjoyably occupied. It is a useful method too for helping with multiplication tables but he needs the appropriate table in front of him while he is listening so that he associates what he is hearing with what he is seeing. If he could trace over the numbers and symbols with his finger at the same time, this will serve to re-enforce the learning process.

REMEDIAL LESSONS WITHIN THE SYLLABUS
If extra help is arranged for your child, try to arrange it so that he doesn't miss the subjects he is good at. For example, if he is good at art or craft or games, he should not be having his remedial lesson at these times. He needs to show how good he is at these subjects and be in a situation where he can be praised. It is much better to arrange the remedial lesson when the remainder of the class are having an English lesson. In some cases children have given up French because it has proved to be too difficult, and they have their remedial lesson when the others are having French. Of course, if the dyslexic is finding that he can cope with a second language, then he should be given every encouragement.

It is also rather unfair to expect a young child in particular to have an extra lesson after school or even on a Saturday morning. He will be tired at the end of the day and possibly exhausted by the end of the week and will need the weekend to 're-charge' and pursue his own interests.

Don't insist he reads to you every evening either. If he asks and wants to read to you that is fine, but I feel very sorry for a child when I hear a parent say "I insist he reads to me for half an hour or even more every night". I try to put a stop to that if I possibly can and suggest games that can be played instead. Some of these are listed in the next chapter which is part of a lecture I gave in August 1979 at the conference "The Dyslexic Child in School" at Keeble College.

JOIN YOUR LOCAL SOCIETY
Finally it is important to join your local Dyslexia Society. You will find the members very helpful, and a useful source of information. They have a great deal of knowledge and will advise you. Each Dyslexia Society holds its own meetings and you will get to know other parents with similar problems. Local Societies and addresses of secretaries are listed at the end of the book. This was accurate at the time this book went to print.

Above all, keep your sense of humour and don't look on dyslexia as a disaster, nor as a disease which can be cured. Agreed it is a nuisance in a society where one seems to be judged largely on one's ability to read and write well, but it is one which can be overcome with the correct attitude and the right sort of help.

GAMES AND ACTIVITIES FOR PARENTS AND CHILDREN TO PLAY

Games and activities play a very important part in the development of a child. Not only are they socially and emotionally useful but they help to prepare a child for his formal learning. Unfortunately, many children entering school today seem to have missed out on the pre-school games which their parents enjoyed in play-grounds and streets. Maybe this is partly due to television and today s more sophisticated toys, but whatever the reasons, much imaginative and repetitive play seems to have been lost. Consequently, concepts such as grouping, rhyming and orientation are not fully understood. When children find it difficult to read and spell it may be because they have not had enough early learning experiences.

STRUGGLING WITH READING
When parents become aware that a child is struggling with reading, naturally they want to help as much as possible. Unfortunately, often they try to do this by asking the child to read a page or more from his reading book every evening. If the child is willing to read there is no problem, but in my experience this is the exception rather than the rule. More commonly both parent and child soon become frustrated and the child resentful and bored with the whole business of reading.

Parents are usually far too emotionally involved with their children to be impartial teachers. It is preferable therefore that learning should take place in a more relaxed and informal atmosphere which is generated by playing games. The following are suggestions for activities which I have found useful, both in the home as the mother of dyslexic sons, and also as a teacher in the classroom and with remedial groups. Remember, however, that games are meant to be enjoyed. If the child is not willing, do not force him. Nothing will be achieved.

MAKING LEARNING ENJOYABLE

1 Say nursery rhymes together. Lately these seem to have gone out of fashion and have been sorely neglected. They are part of our heritage and help to encourage an awareness of rhythm and rhyme at an early age.

2 Read poetry to your children, especially amusing or nonsense poems. Try making up jingles and limericks together.

3 Mime a particular nursery rhyme or incident and encourage the child to guess the mime. He can then choose something to mime in return. This encourages children to use new words to describe actions.

4 Play charades in groups.

5 Read to your child. Try and sit side by side so that he can see the script. Move your finger underneath the words as you read them. If you know you are going to be very busy, tape some stories in advance. The Ladybird books, both fiction and fact, are a very good source of material.

It is helpful to read slowly and clearly so that the child can follow the script as he listens to the tape. It helps some children if a small but distinctive sound is recorded when the end of each page is reached, indicating that it is time to turn over. The child who has lost his place can then start following again on the next page. When your child is older you may well have to help him to cope with reading, even at Secondary level, especially for book reviews and revision.

6 Provide pictures to talk about. Help the child to notice the way in which prepositions are used in discussion. "Is the man in the blue hat *in front of* or *behind* the lady?" "Is the boy climbing *under* or *over* the gate?" "Is the bus going *up* or *down* the hill?"

7 Outings to interesting places — the zoo, museums, the airport. A child who may be missing out on general knowledge because he is behind with reading can learn a great deal from such visits.

8 Hunt the thimble. Encourage the child to verbalise using prepositions again. Is the thimble *inside* the pot, *under* the pot, *on* the box, etc.

9 Playground games, e.g., Follow my leader. In and out among the bluebells. The ally ally O.

10 The Hokey Cokey. This will help to develop a feeling for 'left' and 'right'.

11 Board games, e.g., Snakes and Ladders and Ludo, which are not only enjoyable in themselves but require counters to be moved in a certain direction in a systematic way.

12 Bingo, which helps visual perception.

13 Watching television *together*. Television can be a useful form of learning provided it is not allowed to be passive. Programmes such as Play School, Play Away and Blue Peter offer a great deal of scope for

further discussion and activities. Older children enjoy factual programmes involving nature study and exploration which can lead on to project work and interest files.

14 There are some splendid puzzle books in book shops and stationers. Make use of these — joining dots, and following mazes, encourage good hand-eye control. 'Spot the difference' encourages attention to detail and the use of visual memory.

15 Encourage your child to help in the kitchen — making tea or a simple sponge. Both need to be carried out in a set order if a successful end product is to be accomplished.

LISTENING ACTIVITIES AND AUDITORY SEQUENCING

1 Put various objects in containers — sand, dried peas, pennies, buttons, etc. Shake the containers one at a time and ask the child to say what he thinks might be inside and describe the sound. Ask him questions, "Is there one penny in here or more than one? Is the sound hard? gentle? soft?

2 Listening to everyday sounds, preferably with eyes closed. What can be heard? The telephone ringing, hammering, voices, a clock ticking.

Listen to household sounds, e.g., hoover, food mixer, washing machine, spin drier.

Listen to traffic sounds — motor bike, lorry, ambulance, car, etc.

3 Tape some everyday sounds, e.g., tap dripping, toilet flushing, phone ringing. Play them to the child and see if he can recognise them. Learning Development Aids' Sound Lotto and Sound Stories are very useful and enjoyable activities.

4   Ask the child to close his eyes and guess who is speaking. Is it Mother? Sister? Grandma? Auntie?

5   Tap or clap a simple rhythm for the child to repeat. Gradually make the rhythms more difficult. Clap words with two or more syllables. Say the word as you clap, e.g., black-board, hol-i-day, ra-di-a-tor. Later, give the child a word to clap. Can he say how many beats the word has?

6   "I Spy". This game is too difficult for some children if the letter names are used. Therefore, take it in stages and play it several ways.

   a)   Using the *sound*, e.g., I spy with my little eye something beginning with the sound (b)

   b)   Increase the load, e.g., I spy with my little eye something beginning with the same sound as "ball"

   c)   Using the *letter name*, e.g., I spy with my little eye something beginning with the letter B

   d)   Using *rhyming*. I spy with my little eye something that rhymes with bat

   e)   *Ending sound*. I spy with my little eye something *ending* with the sound (b).

7   *Sound* a word in individual units, e.g., m-a-n, and ask the child to say whole word man. Increase the number of sounds in the word, e.g., l-a-m-p, t-r-u-m-p-e-t.

8   **Rhyming.** Start off the round with a word and ask each person to say a rhyming word, e.g., day — play — may — tray. The first to break the rhyme must start a new round, e.g., pin — tin — thin, etc.

9 "Simon (or O'Grady) says". Start with very simple instructions and gradually make them more difficult, e.g., Simon says touch your *left* ear with your *right* hand.

10 Say a group of words with a "stranger" in it, e.g., cat, dog, apple, fox. The child tells you or draws a picture of the stranger. This can also be played with rhyming words, e.g., cat, bat, fox, hat. Which word didn't rhyme? Also with words which begin with the same sound, e.g. pig, pat, bin, peg. Which is the odd one?

11 I went to market and I bought. . . .
Start with a particular group of things, e.g., fruit or vegetables, because it is easier for the child to remember related things. Later, shop for random items, e.g., a piano, a thimble, tablemats, a fur coat, etc.

This game can also be played where each item must begin with a given letter, e.g., peas, potatoes, pancakes, etc.

Vary the game with other beginnings, e.g.,
I packed my case with. . . .
In my Christmas stocking I found. . . .
On my birthday I had. . . .

12 Songs involving memory and sequencing, e.g.
Old MacDonald had a farm
The Twelve Days of Christmas
Ten Green Bottles
Songs and rhymes involving days of the week and months of the year.

13 Following instructions: Start with two only, e.g., "Please pick up the pencil and put it in the box."

Gradually make the sequence longer, e.g., "Go to the cupboard, take out a green exercise book, write your name on the front, bring it to me."

14 As soon as the child can sequence the alphabet, ask him to arrange wooden alphabet letters on the table in the shape of a rainbow.

Say a sequence of letters to him, e.g., M D S. Ask him to repeat the sequence and then to take out the letters from the rainbow and arrange them in the order in which he said them. Increase the number of letters, one at a time.

LOOKING ACTIVITIES AND VISUAL SEQUENCING
1 Snap. Use pictures only at first then, perhaps, introduce letters and words.

2 Pairs.

3 Pelmanism or memory games.

4 Dominoes.

5 Sorting things into colours, shapes and sizes.

Sorting pictures, e.g., put all the pictures which begin with the same sound as table in one pile, and all the pictures which begin with the same sound as dog in another pile.

6 Happy Families.

7 Look together at a picture. Cover the picture and ask the child questions about it, e.g., How many children were in the picture? How many people were wearing hats? Was it winter or summer?

8 Provide a tray of objects for the child to look at.

After a few seconds cover the tray and ask him to name all the objects he saw.

9 Provide a tray of objects. Ask the child to close his eyes. One or more objects are then removed from the tray. Ask the child to open his eyes and say which objects he thinks were removed.

10 Draw three shapes on a card, show the card to the child, cover it, and then ask him to draw what he saw. Gradually increase the difficulty of the shapes and the length of the sequence.

11 Show the child several pictures — three is enough at first, and ask him to arrange them in order to make a story. Encourage him to tell you the story or speak it on to a tape recorder. He may even be able to write it down.

12 Draw several related pictures and include a stranger, e.g., apple, pear, book, plum. Ask the child to point to the "odd man out".

13 If the child knows his alphabet letters, put several out on the table and ask him to look at them for a few seconds, cover them and ask him to write down or say which ones he saw.

14 Ask him to arrange his alphabet in the shape of a rainbow. Show him a card with three letters on it, e.g., S B X. Remove the card and ask him to take out the letters he saw and place them in the order in which he saw them. This is a *looking* activity. Do not say the name of the letters.

15 Bingo — looking only.

LEARNING THROUGH TOUCH

1 Tracing shapes, letters, words, simple pictures, etc.

2 Making letters with plasticene, modelling clay or pipe cleaners. Using chalk, paint, thick felt pens to write very large letters. Making letters with the forefinger in a tray of dry sand.

3 Feeling and naming sandpaper or felt letters with eyes closed.

4 Feeling and naming wooden letters with eyes closed.

5 Put various objects or wooden letters in bags and ask the child to name the object or letter.

6 Jigsaw puzzles.

7 Thread a sequence of coloured beads on to a string and ask the child to repeat the sequence several times.

PHYSICAL SKILLS

Do not neglect the physical skills, such as throwing, catching and kicking balls, skipping, hopping and jumping. Many children find these activities difficult and will need a great deal of practice.

A word of warning about commercially produced word games, such as "Scrabble": They are designed for good spellers, and are rarely enjoyed by weak spellers. To put a child in a position where he feels stupid or slow, especially in front of younger siblings, is unforgivable.

There are, however, many excellent learning games and activities on the market now from publishers, such as "Learning Development Aids" and "Living and Learning". In many cases, however, home-made games can be made with the help of the child who can draw or cut out the pictures. It is a good idea to base home-made games on commercial games already familiar to the child, e.g., Snap, Pelmanism, Snakes and Ladders.

When making games, several questions should be asked:

1 Is the game fair?
2 Does it contain elements of both skill and luck?
3 Are the rules simple enough to be easily understood?
4 If it is a learning game, is it self-checking?
5 If it is a learning game, is it actually achieving its aim?

EXAMPLES OF HOME-MADE GAMES

1 *Three in a Row* – a game for two players.
   Requirements: One piece of cardboard roughly 28 cm
   square, divided into nine equal squares, two sets of
   coloured counters and a pack of small cards with
   words on one side and pictures on the other.

   The rules of the game are the same as noughts and
   crosses.

   For reading: Place nine small cards, word side
   uppermost on the large card. The first player points to
   the word he wishes to read, reads it, turns the card
   over to check with the picture that he is correct, and if
   so, he places a counter on the top of the card. The
   second player then plays. The first player to get "three
   in a row" is the winner.

   For spelling: Place the small cards on the large card
   picture uppermost. First player points to the picture of
   the word he wants to spell, says the word, spells it (or
   writes it down), and turns the card over to check with
   the word that he is correct. If so, he places a counter
   on it and a second player plays.

   In the case of a player not being able to read or spell
   a word, the word is discussed and then replaced by a
   different word. Include the "tricky" word again when
   the next nine cards are selected.

2 *First to a hundred* – a game for 2, 3, or 4 players. This game must be supervised by an adult or good reader or have a check list accompanied with illustrations.

Requirements: A Snakes and Ladders board, a dice, counters and a pack of cards with words printed on one side. Place the cards in a pile, word side down. Play as for Snakes and Ladders, but before the player moves his counter he must pick up a word and read it. If correct, he keeps the card. If not, the word is read for him and then put at the bottom of the pack to come up again. "First to a hundred" is the winner.

3 *Four in One* – so called because the pack of cards can be used to play four games each with 2, 3, or 4 players.

Requirements: Blank playing cards. Make a "family" for each letter of the alphabet:

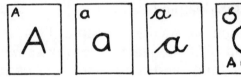

These cards can then be used for adaptations of standard games:

1 *Snap* Any of the following can be snapped:
   - Any two upper case letters
   - Any two lower case letters
   - Any two written letters
   - Any two clue pictures
   - Any two of the same family.

2 *Happy Families* – Deal seven cards to each player and play in the normal way, asking: "(Name) have you the capital A of the A family?"
   or .... have you the small letter of the A family?
   .... have you the written letter of the A family?
   .... have you the clue picture of the A family?

3 *Pairs* – Deal five cards and play as for Happy Families
   but collecting only two of any family.

4 *Pelmanism* (The "Memory" Game) – Choose any six or
   eight families and place face down on the table. Play
   in the normal way. Any two cards of a family are a set.

   For some children in particular the actual physical
   participation of card games is very important —
   looking and listening carefully, repeating, sounding
   out, turning cards over, grouping, remembering and
   recalling.

An inventive mother or teacher will probably make
additions to these games and I hope will find them as
helpful with children as I did when I made them for my
sons over twelve years ago. I have used them over and
over again since with children who need constant
repetition in their learning.

Soon after writing this section on games I was reading
the second part of Dirk Bogarde's autobiography entitled
"Snakes and Ladders" and came across this passage. It is
included by kind permission of the publishers Chatto
and Windus.

. . . .I finally became a fully qualified Air Photographic
Interpreter and was ordered to leave my furious
Brigadier to report urgently to London. Air Photographic
Interpretation (the reading of aerial Photographs taken
from a height of anything between 1,000 to 30,000
feet) is very much a question, in simple terms, of
observation, an eye for detail, and memory. I was
happily possessed, to a modest degree, of all three, due
in the main, I feel sure, to an apparently witless game
my father made us play as children. In a shop window
how many pots and pans, how many with lids, how
many without? How many tea pots, plates with blue
rims, jugs with pink roses? Make a mental list, look away

for a moment or two, look back and check. In the Underground, look at the people opposite. Memorize the faces. Look at the feet. Look away. Who had the bunion, the toe-caps, the brogues, spats, lace-ups or buttons? Even the breakfast table was not spared. After a good look one closed one's eyes while he very slightly disarranged the setting. Look again. Was the label on the marmalade facing you before? Was there a lump of sugar in the tea spoon? Had the milk jug turned its back? Two or three pieces of toast in the rack?

I had no idea that this childhood game would one day prove to be the key to a life in a war; without it I would very likely have had my twenty-four hours (or whatever it was) life expectation as an Infantry Officer and that would have been that. As it was I became a moderately accomplished specialist in an extremely complicated branch of Army Intelligence for the remainder of my service. And no one was more surprised than I, or more delighted. I loved the detail, the intense concentration, the working out of problems, the searching for clues and above all the memorizing. It was, after all, a very theatrical business. How many haystacks had there been in that field three weeks ago? Look back and check. Six. Now there were sixteen. . . did the tracks lead *to* them and not *away* from them? Were they made by tracked vehicles or wheeled ones? Guns, tanks or radar maybe? Or were they, after all, only haystacks, it was June. . . but the tracks led inwards. A hay cart would have been parallel and left turning-loops. . . these ended in the little stacks. Too short for tanks, too round for trucks. . . probably 88mm guns. . . a long, silent, painstaking job.

RECOGNISING THE PROBLEM IN SCHOOL

I should say first of all that a child who is slow to read is not necessarily dyslexic. Children fail to read for many reasons, low intellectual ability, emotional disturbance, lack of maturity, poor physical attributes, e.g. poor eye-sight or hearing, intermittent or catarrhal deafness. Many immature children make mistakes similar to those made by a dyslexic e.g. reversing b's and d's and reading 'was' for 'saw' etc., but with developing maturity these children grow out of their problem by 7½ or 8. The dyslexic however does not. He continues to make these mistakes into his teens and beyond.

FIRST IN JUNIOR SCHOOL
The dyslexic child in the reception class may be the one who puts his coat on back to front or inside out. When he does get it on he finds difficulty in fastening it up with the button in the appropriate button-hole.

He may not be able to tie his shoe laces and may repeatedly put his shoes on the wrong feet. He probably won't be able to do up his tie.

He may get his words mixed up or have a slight lisp or impediment. He may be ambilateral i.e. not show a preference for either hand. For some things he uses his right hand and for some his left. He may appear to be right handed one day and left handed the next. He may be clumsy and "accident prone". He may not be able to remember what day it is or when his birthday is. He does not seem to understand time of day and may be unable to read the clock. He may not be able to skip or hop, clap rhythms, throw, catch or kick a ball. He will probably have great difficulty copying particularly from the blackboard and will ignore punctuation for reading and writing. Many times children copy letter by letter from the blackboard but have no idea what they have written.

At first he may be able to remember a few "Look and Say" words for reading but once the load increases he will forget them all. He may not be able to recognise a word a second after he has been told what it is. If he has poor visual perception he will confuse letters which look alike. He may find sounds difficult to learn if he has poor auditory skills and will not easily distinguish between similar sounds and in particular the vowel sounds. He may become confused between the names and the sounds of the letters and may not be able to blend sounds together.

He may have difficulty saying the days of the week, or the months of the year in order, and in learning his tables. Almost all dyslexics will have difficulty remembering things in sequence, for example, carrying out a series of instructions. When sent to shop for only two items, a dyslexic often returns with something entirely different or maybe nothing at all.

When the dyslexic child starts writing, he will probably confuse all the ball and stick letters b d p g q. It seems the policy in nearly all first schools to let children print, and only later on to teach handwriting. I cannot see the logic of this. Miss Kathleen Hickey in her excellent book "Dyslexia — A Language Training Course for Teachers and Learners" advocates that children learn to write from the beginning with an approach stroke and a lead-off stroke to each letter. This helps the child to progress easily to "joined up" writing. To achieve this the child learns to write in definite and distinct steps. First he learns to write the letter over the top of the printed form, saying the sound and name of the letter as he writes it, hence re-enforcing the association between the sound and name and shape of the letter in particular the relationship between the printed form and the written form. In this way the ball and stick letters have different shapes and are not so easily confused for writing, e.g., instead of b d p g q the written shapes are:

$$b \; d \; p \; g \; q$$

The dyslexic child may also confuse writing of numbers. 5 for 3, or 5 for 2, 3 for 8, 6 for 9 or 7 for 4.

In addition to numbers giving problems, mathematical signs can also be confusing. There is very little difference visually between $+$ and $\times$, $<$ and $>$, $=$ and $\div$.

Learning tables may also be difficult and is not essential. It is much better for the child to aim for an automatic response to 9 x 9's or 6 x 2's. This can be done by using a table chart frequently, or by the use of games.

A child with some or all of these problems will make little progress in reading in the first school and less in spelling. His written work will probably be very poor and the teacher may well have noticed a discrepancy between his oral ability and his written work.

IN MIDDLE SCHOOL
When the child reaches the middle school he may have started reading but his written work will not be good. He may well have great difficulty getting his thoughts on to paper. There will be many wrong spellings and crossings out. He will still be reversing his letters and perhaps confusing the names and sounds of letters. Reading aloud will be difficult and he may do so very

hesitantly and inaccurately, losing his place often, missing out lines or re-reading the same line twice. He will possibly leave out letters and syllables in words.

Even when he can break up a word correctly into several syllables he may not then retain the order of the syllables to put them back together to read the whole word correctly.

Although his reading age is probably behind his expected ability, often such a child may be unable to obtain any extra help in school for numerous reasons. His written English makes little or no improvement and he will become increasingly disheartened. In secondary school even an intelligent dyslexic is likely to experience difficulties. He is often still a slow reader and his written work frequently unstructured and full of reversals, additions, omissions and transpositions. Some of these look like careless errors, so that he is then regarded as being just that, a careless boy who produces messy, untidy work with numerous crossings out and little or no punctuation. Often the work is handed in unfinished.

IN SECONDARY SCHOOL
Dyslexic children in secondary school need positive help in organising their work. They also need to be specifically taught language structure which includes spelling choices, rules, grammar and punctuation. Some examining boards allow extra time in public examinations but if the school has not prepared the child for this extra time allowance, it is of little benefit to him for he will not know how to use it profitably.

A secondary school child will experience great difficulty taking notes and dictation because it is hard for him to listen and write at the same time. There will be gaps in his work making revision impossible.

Copying from the blackboard will continue to be a problem. He will lose his place and either omit words or write them twice. If homework assignments are put up on the blackboard they may well be copied down incorrectly or incompletely, perhaps resulting in the wrong work being done or only part of the work being done.

Sometimes a series of instructions are given at the beginning of a lesson, e.g. "Take out your text book, turn to page 69. Read through the passage giving the description of 'Autumn' and answer questions 9 – 13". Confronted by a sequence like this, the dyslexic child may be totally confused and not even remember the first instruction. This then looks as if he wasn't paying attention and he probably gets into trouble for not listening.

Some dyslexics continue to say words in the wrong order. I teach a 40 year old man who constantly refers to "one syllable words" as "one word syllables". He also has difficulty getting his tongue round multi-syllabic words. He says 'necesselery' for 'necessarily' and 'catipal letter' for 'capital letter'.

HANDWRITING SPACING
Apart from poor handwriting spacing is often poor. There may be large gaps between letters but no gaps between words. There may however, be huge gaps between words where the child is only writing three or four words per line. He may also find difficulty keeping close to the margin so he starts with a full line at the top of the page but only half a line at the bottom.

Fusion is also quite common, e.g. a for ai, a for ar, gh for gh.

HOW TEACHERS CAN HELP IN THE CLASSROOM

It may well be difficult for you to give a dyslexic child the amount of help he needs to improve substantially his written language skills, but there are many things which can be done to make his day more tolerable.

- First of all check that he knows the sounds, names and shapes of all the alphabet letters and that he can recognise the letter in all its forms, i.e. the capital or upper case, the lower case and the written form, e.g. $Bb\mathit{b}$ and that a certain letter has a certain sound (b).

- Check that he knows and can discriminate between the vowel sounds, and that he knows the difference between short and long vowels.

- Check that he understands how to make sounds properly and can blend them together.

- Appreciate that he has difficulty sequencing and that this will account for his not being able to say the days of the week in the correct order, or the months of the year. It will also be the reason why he has difficulty in carrying out instructions.

- Appreciate also that direction is worrying for him and he may often lose his way and get lost, with the result that he will arrive late for lessons, etc. He may not even know which is the beginning of his book.

- Understand that he may take a long time to learn to tell the time and even when he can he may misread the clock.

- When his reading begins to improve don't expect his spelling to improve at the same rate — it won't.

● Don't give him lists of mixed spellings to learn. If he has to be given a list, make it short and preferably choose a family of words, e.g. the 'igh' words or the 'tion' words. *Never* give him lists like:

tough	thief
ought	receive
through	seize
though	chief
bought	neighbour
thought	weigh
enough	heifer
cough	foreign
	rein
	reign
	neither

These are far too confusing. He may spend hours trying to learn them but won't succeed.

● Don't expect him to learn his tables easily and be able to say them. He will not be able to remember the sequence and will lose track in the middle and become very confused. Instead make him a table chart and allow him to use it. Devise games which encourage an automatic response.

● Don't expect him to copy accurately from the blackboard. He will not be able to hold the whole word in his mind so will have to look up for nearly every letter, often losing his place as he does so. If he *has* to copy from the blackboard make sure that the writing he is copying from is clear. If the copying is information needed for homework, check that he has in fact copied it correctly, particularly if page numbers are involved so that he doesn't waste his time working on page 31 when the homework was on page 13. If he has incomplete notes perhaps he could borrow a book from a child who writes neatly and could be given time to make up his notes. He is going to have a hard enough time revising before exams without having to contend with incomplete notes, and remarks like "these notes are incomplete" or "finish this" are not very constructive.

- If there is a class outing try not to give a prize for the best diary or account of the day. If there must be a prize, make it for attitude or helpfulness. So many times the dyslexic doesn't stand a chance of winning the prize, but he might if the competition doesn't rely on written work.

- Don't force him to read aloud in front of his peers. It will be an ordeal for him and he will stumble and hesitate. If he does wish to try, allow him time to prepare the piece first — it may not be perfect but won't be quite so painful for him and the listeners.

- Don't insist he learns a foreign language or music unless he shows some aptitude.

- Never hold his work up to ridicule or compare him with a brother, sister or peer.

- Don't put red marks all over his written work. It is very discouraging. When a word is spelt wrongly it is helpful to underline just the little bit that is wrong so that the child knows where to look. If he is just told the word is wrong he probably won't know what is wrong with it or how to put it right. At least if part of it is underlined he will know which bit to look at again. In subjects such as history or science don't deduct marks for inaccurate spelling. Give the grade on content.

- Appreciate that a dyslexic's work is erratic and shows inconsistencies. Sometimes he can spell a word correctly and sometimes he can't. On occasions a word is spelt in three or four different ways on the same page. Understand that written work will take him a long time and he will often need extra time allowance, particularly for comprehension passages or creative writing.

- Teach him to sequence the alphabet correctly to use his dictionary efficiently. Don't expect him to use a dictionary to find out how to spell a word because he will tell you that you need to know how to spell it first. It is true that at first you do need to know how to spell a word before you can find it. He will need to be taught how to divide up the dictionary efficiently. He needs to be told the obvious things, e.g. that the two words at the top of the page are the first and last words in heavy print. Before he actually uses the dictionary give him lots of work on the sequencing of alphabet letters, first individual letters, then two letters with the first one the same then three letters with the first two the same, e.g.

      a n b c f x,
      sl sa se sn sm,
      sta str ste stu sto.

This leads on to words on cards and finally to the dictionary. Present the child with a word that you want him to find printed clearly on a card, e.g.

stamp

and ask him to find it.

- Do not ask a child to copy his work out again. It will be very tiring for him and may not be any better than the first time.

  Help him to structure his creative writing by making a plan first with a beginning, middle and ending. This applies to children of all ages whether they are writing simple stories or lengthy essays.

- When punishments have to be given, try not to give punishments that require writing, e.g. lines, or copying a page from a dictionary or telephone directory. These are soul-destroying occupations for anyone, but even more so for the dyslexic.

- If you are able to spend some time with him alone or in a small group do so. Bring kinaesthetic and tactile awareness into his learning. Give plenty of visual and auditory discrimination exercises and practice in listening for particular sounds in all positions of words, beginning, middle and end.

- Spend time on blends both initial and final. Work on vowel discrimination and the differences between the sounds of the short and long vowels. Give exercises to improve both visual and auditory sequential memory span. Spend time on sequencing exercises, accenting, rhythm and rhyming. Teach him spelling choices, rules for adding affixes, word patterns and syllable division. He will not pick these things up from reading — they will have to be taught to him together with much opportunity for over-learning and re-enforcement.

- Explain to him points which seem to be obvious, e.g. No *English* word ends with j — use ge or dge. No *English* word ends with v — always ve. No *English*

word ends with i — use y. No *English* word ends
with qu. Longer endings follow short vowels, e.g. tch,
dge, ll, ff, ck. Every syllable must have at least one
one vowel.

● Lastly, if you, the teacher, feel that the child has a
real problem and you have not the time or the
experience to deal with it, make sure the child is
referred for extra tuition by a specialist teacher with
whom you should keep in close touch. The child is
in your hands — you must not let him down.

POINTS TO LOOK FOR
i) Persistent difficulty with letters which look alike, e.g.

b d p g q
r n h b
i t l j
h y
t f j
m ω   MW
n u
s z   SZ

ii) Difficulty with sounds which are similar

(ă) (ŏ) (ŭ)   (ĭ) (ĕ)   (f) (th)
(ē) (ĭ)   (v) (t̲h̲)
(m) (n)   (d) (t)

(p) (b)   (g) (k)
(s) (z)   (n) (ng)
(j) (ch)   (ch) (tr) (dr)
(j) (dr)   (cr) (kw)

This results in spellings such as:

cad	for	cut
sid	for	sit
sop	for	shop
chree	for	tree
wiv	for	with

iii) Confusion with the names and sounds of letters, e.g.:

nd	for	end
flt	for	felt
tmpr	for	temper
ne	for	any
tch	for	teacher
snd	for	send
mrch	for	march
tnt	for	tent
fl	for	fell
hlp	for	help

iv) Confusion between t and l

teller	for	letter
filler	for	fitter
tiller	for	litter
little	for	title

An intelligent dyslexic will begin to devise his own methods of coping. He will use capital b's and d's because he is more certain which is correct, e.g. raBBit, coBweB, cuDDle, miDDle.

If he is confused between i and e he may write *è*

If he is confused between *σ* and *α* he may write *α*

Ball and stick letters become d ⊕ ⊕ ⊕ ⊕

j and g confusion results in **ġ**

Similar sounding words may be very confusing

e.g.,	accept	and	except
	affect	and	effect
	heroic	and	erotic
	shoulder	and	soldier
	our	and	are
	once	and	wants
	one	and	won

Similar looking words also, e.g.:

where, there, here   who, whom, whose
how, who, why   at, to   for, from, off

Letters in words will often be written in the wrong order. I recently had "being" for "begin" "tierd" for "tired" "sign" for "sing".

These were all in the same paragraph.

Dyslexics do not always hear both letters in a blend so they write:

had	for	hand
ten	for	tent
lap	for	lamp
tap	for	trap

Telescoping of syllables is common resulting in the following mistakes for reading and writing:

affectly	for	affectionately
conversion	for	conversation
grandly	for	gradually
possibly	for	possibility

It is important that all English teachers recognise these types of error and also inform all teachers of other subjects about them.

EXAMPLES OF WORK BY DYSLEXIC STUDENTS

The following section contains examples of work from dyslexic students aged 7 – 40 years of age. All are of at least average intelligence.

They contain the types of error explained in the chapter entitled "Recognising the problem in school".

This is an eight year old girl's illustration of a policeman *stopping* the traffic. I have shown it to many dyslexic children. They see nothing wrong with it.

FOUR EXAMPLES OF HOW <u>NOT</u> TO TREAT CHILDREN'S EFFORTS.

Example 1.

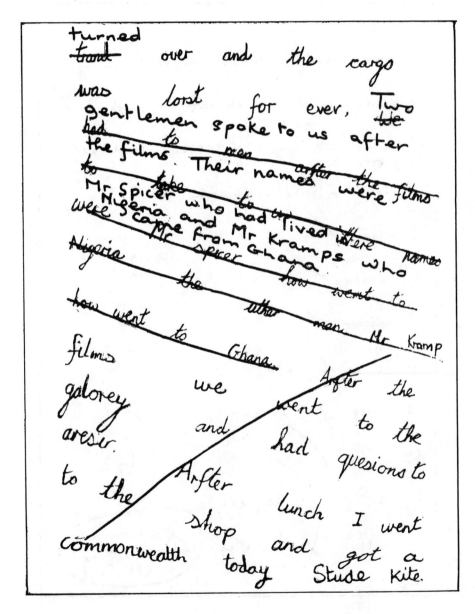

Example 2.

1 wekness Weakness 13 linger ✓

2 likeness ✓ likely   14 ~~tafed~~ laughed ✗

3 ~~lttel~~ likieley ✗   15 ~~taffes~~. laghter ✗

4 lonly ✗ lonely   16 ~~tafe~~ lahgf ✗

5 inform ✓

6 victory ✓

7 visitor ✓

8 moter ✗ motor

9 louly ✗ lovely

10 nicely ✓

11 safly ✗ safely

   latly ✗ lately

laugh

laughed

laughter

6

Disgusting!

Example 3.

1. ~~said~~ cought ✗
2. thought ✗
3. Tought ✗
4. clough ✗
5. bort ✗
6. laugh ✓
7. otaught ✗
8. baugh ✗
9. brort ✗
10. Rough ✗

$\frac{1}{10}$

learn again
— tomorrow !

Example 4.

A nine year old dyslexic girl with a reading age of 10 years.

Frost

Frost is relly ~~frozan~~ vaper that has landed in the night and frozen. In the morning every thing is frozen and looks very beutifull but when it melts it is the same old ordeny thing. If you look at a Spiders web when it is Prosan it looks very butifull and it glisans. If there is water on the ground it avaporats and goes in to the air and in to the clouds there it thurns in to water and fresers and at night it comes down as mist and lands and in the morning it looks like wright pourder and it is very skidy. Puddlers will frers in the night but in a fue owers it will turn to water agian.

All these words 10 times each please in your work book! (Please!)

frozen   vapour   beautiful
ordinary   glistens   evaporates
white   few hours.

Frost is really frozen vapour that has landed in the night and frozen. In the morning everything is frozen and looks very beautiful but when it melts it is the same old ordinary thing. If you look at a spider's web when it is frozen, it looks very beautiful and it glistens. If there is water on the ground it evaporates and goes into the air and into the clouds, there it turns into water and freezes and at night it comes down as mist and lands and in the morning it looks like white powder and it is very skiddy. Puddles will freeze in the night but in a few hours it will turn to water again.

Example 5.
An eight and a half year old boy's attempt to write the alphabet and his name. Note the fusions.

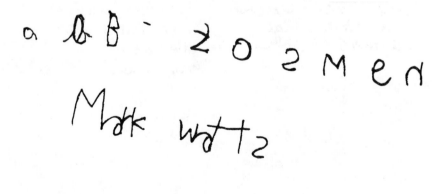

A few months later after following the language structure and multi-sensory techniques advocated by Kathleen Hickey:

but oll the trid, hod the sghehm ahd then tha oll uent dehd. the rev ahd tha gand a got print oyp a tigu ahd one op the mah sed it musde a mah lt eatung tigu so that hit oll op the vid lot the plos up and uuer the tigu cluuss he

. . .but all the tribe
had the signal
and then they
all went down to
the river and
they found a
foot print
of a tiger
and one
of the men
said, "it must be
a man eating
tiger"
So that night
all of the tribe
locked the place
up and when
the tiger
comes he. . .

101

Two years later.

jim and the u.g.o
) one day jim was at school. he was looking out og the window day dream ing when from out og no where came a u.g.o.
He poot up his hand to tell the teacher but the teacher did not bleve him she said "stop tooking rubbish, get on whith yor work!"
The bell went got home time and on the way home he spoke to no - one becos he got that thay wod think he was mad when he got home he went up to his bedroom and looked out og the window. he was staggered to see that the u.g.o. had landld

(ē) = ea
(öö) = oo (ö) u
(ē) ea.
(sĕd) = said ru'|bish
because thought would

The margin at the side is for "helpful clues". "Because", "thought" and "would" are sight words which he later worked on, using the whole word multisensory technique.

Example 6.

Jonathon, aged eight years.

Life   in   a   maner howse

They   played   so   games, ∧ chess
~~kites~~ Lites   end   for   the   girl they played
with   Dolles   ~~They~~ ther   ~~bedes~~ beds   ere
                      dolls   *Their*
made   of   woed   with polles
to   put   ther   ~~cloves~~ on .
                                   clothes
In   the   lower   holl   they
have had   ~~they~~ their   diner   they   eat
welf with   ~~they~~ their   hendes . ~~they~~ hair
                                   hands   *The*
or   boyes   are is   ~~awees~~ shof
                                           always
end   the   girles   hair   is ~~logs~~
                                                       long
~~an~~   ~~n~~   ~~a~~ ~~big~~ ~~howse~~
~~they~~ ther   ~~shose~~   ~~or~~   ~~girles~~   are pointed .
       Their *shoes*

See me

Example 6 continued

Jonathon's sister at the same age.

My ~~birday~~ Adventu
I rom away from hame
and found that ~~we~~ I had
gon thonu a ~~thon~~ time
Slipe and I was in a
difrent world I did not
no what it was but I
hode a filing some one
was foling me the peple
were like us and food wa
pleteful so was water th
peple were frends the hete
was geting hoter and
peple were geting ill
and some were ded and I
was geting hote mg
self I was not get bad
but it was to late in the
night for get medhil
Selplys so we went so
bed and I hale to pole
a tent up before I went tc
bed ~~me toods~~ with me
was mg firnd and I hade
lost a nother firnd we
hade a nufe food to last
4 days and nghts

Jonathon's sister, now fifteen, wrote out the passage
again for the purpose of the book. Note the spellings of
friend — correct on line 7 but incorrect twice on line
14. Also *diferent* for different and *surplies* for supplies.

My holiday Adventure.
I ran away from home and I found that I had
gone through a time slip and I was in a
diferent world. I did not know what it was
but I had a feeling someone was following
me. The people were like us and the food
was plentiful. So was water. The people were
friends. The heat was getting hotter and
people were getting ill and some were dead.
And I was getting hot myself. I was
not get bad but it was too late in the
night for get medical surplies. So we
went to bed and I had to put a tent
up before I went to bed. With me was
my freind and I had lost another freind.
We had enough food to last for four
days and nights.

Example 7.

An example of an eight and a half year old boy copying letter by letter from the blackboard. He was unable to read the words and had no idea what he had written.

The red bud fell on the wet mud us the ant ron ond hid fi Hecon not ge tint the Well the man dag for the lid is on on it

Example 8.

A twelve year old boy's attempt to write the days of the week.

Thesday
Thosday
Wednesday
Monday
Satday
Freday
Sunday

Example 9.

A dyslexic boy aged nine years. Note the complete lack of punctuation and the maximum of only four words on a line, also the inability to stay close to the margin.

Jim   lived   in   a
littel   house   nere   a
river .
One   day   Jim   went
for   a   walk   in
the   forist   but   he
got   lost   then   he
Saw   a   cave   thats
Stranj   he   Siad
then   he   fell   in
were   am   I   he
Siad   Hello   who   are
you   Siad   a   vosce
Jim   taned   rawed
I   am   Jim   Siad
Jim   and   I   fell
thruo   that   holl
I   carn   get
you   back   can
you   Siad   Jim
yes   but   you
will   hafto   get

Example 10.

A 10 year old boy's attempt to write the days of the week, months of the year and numbers to twenty.

monday   thaday   vendau

thaday   Fllday   satday
sunday

tanave   feven   mrach   aprull
may   jun   jly   ogost
setaore November Deseter

1 ane	ⓘ ellevon	
2 tou	② thel3	
3 there	13 thten	
4 fout	16 fourten	
5 five	15) suveten	
6 six	16) sixten	
7 seven	17) seventen	
8 aghlt	18) eghtten	
9 nine	19) nineten	
10 ten	20) twveten	

Example 11.

This story was written by a nine year old girl.

The Dog wie at a nam
one dag There wos a LItll Doy wjeut
annam Sow he wet at to See IF the
Kood Find a ham. he meb a LitU bud
and he ust he iF he Kood hog ne
Fik of a nam Soo he Sed Lasse and
the he Sad yes

The dog without a name.
One day there was a little dog without
a name so he went out to see if he
could find a name. He met a little bird
and he asked him if he could help him
think of a name so he said Lassie and
the dog said "Yes"

Example 12

A twelve year old boy's letter to his twin brother.

Dear Tom,

I got your letter and read your letter. I could come to the boat for two days and the stuff is on the boat and the boat is by the bank, and the boat is a launch. I am sorry I forgot your birthday and I got your birthday box and card.

Example 13

A twenty year old man's description of his job.

I lick werking on car becos of it is my job but it is dterly i werek on qil a slesan of car i manty lick foured but i hav to put up wif mad tipst of cor to werek on but it is verdy denty to dok

The same passage, written for dictation, two months later.

I like working on cars because it is ony job but it is dirty. I work on quite a sedectoon. of cars. I Mainly likes Fords but I have to put up with most types of cats to work on but it is very dirty to dog.

A further month later.

I like working on cars because
it is my job, but it is dirty.

I work on quite a seleson of
cars.

I mainly like Fords but I
have to put up with most
typres of cars to work on
but it is very dirty to
do.

Example 14

Numbers can also be a problem

$$46 \over 32$$ ✓

$$\underline{18}$$ /

add

$$\begin{array}{c} 8 \\ 82 \\ \hline \end{array}$$ 0 R

$$57 \over 40$$ /

$$\overline{7}$$

add

$$55 \over 24$$ ✓

$$\overline{7 R}$$

$$\begin{array}{c} 6\,3 \\ 2\,2 \end{array}$$ ✓

$$\overline{85}$$

add

$$\begin{array}{c} 3\,9 \\ 3\,0 \end{array}$$

$$\overline{5 R} \, 9$$

9   9 99999 9 9 9 9 999999 /

4 sets of 2 → 8 ,

$$5 \times 2 \rightarrow 10$$ ✓

$$7 \times 2 \rightarrow 4\,8$$

$$9 \times 2 \rightarrow 8\,8$$

$$10 \times 2 \rightarrow 2\,4$$

$$3 \times 2 \rightarrow 8$$

$$\begin{array}{r} 8 \\ \times 2 \\ \hline 16 \end{array}$$

$$\begin{array}{r} 11 \\ \times 2 \\ \hline 22 \end{array}$$

$$\begin{array}{r} 5 \\ \times 2 \\ \hline 102 \end{array}$$

$$\begin{array}{r} 4\,3 \\ \times 2 \\ \hline 8\,8 \end{array}$$

$$\begin{array}{r} 8\,2 \\ \times 2 \\ \hline 16\,4 \end{array}$$ ✓

$$\begin{array}{r} 3\,1 \\ \times 2 \\ \hline 1\,2 \end{array}$$

Example 14 continued

```
add          May 19th
2 4          add      add
3 5    ✓     5 3      6 6
5P           3 4      3Ɵ
             8ƒ  ✓    76  ✓
add
4.8₀         add      add
3.0          75       36
78  ✓        21  ✓    52    ✓
             96       8ƀ

add          add              add
1 3          2 4              2 3
2 2          3 0              1 5
3 3  ✓       4 1              3 1
68           145,             6 P  ✓
             P 5  ✓                        ✓

     9  9  9  9  9  9   9  9

  ②  3  4  5  6  ⑦  8  ⑨  10
```

Example 15

This account was written by a boy of twelve and a half years of age who had recently moved to secondary school and was finding it difficult to cope.

My life at School

My life at school is very hard
some techers pick on me or that
vate. I think.
The punishment I have been
given are.
100 lines
Otensmant
Write all my work out angn.
Beiging hit over the head with
a tringl and a book.
Boy pick on me.
The teachers I hate are
all of them exped . . . . . .
I hate my life at school
I think nobody likes me evene
my frens are hordle.
Thinking I find hard too
do are.
Copey from the black board
Doing mathes.
One day I had to do about
3h30 mints homwork.
They is one thing they can-
not take away from me is my
hapnis.
One teacher pu pulled my hair
for singing
I would like to get a mit
mac so I could tell erreone.
There are dolles in the school
trying to trip us up
I think that errthing comes
a part in my hans like I broke
the gom and smash thing.

MY LIFE AT SCHOOL

My life at school is very hard. Some teachers pick on me or that is what I think.

The punishments I have been given are
> 100 lines
> Detention
> Writing all my work out again
> Being hit over the head with a triangle and a book

Boys pick on me.

The teachers I hate are all of them except. . .

I hate my life at school. I think nobody likes me, even my friends are horrible.

Things I find hard to do are
> Copying from the blackboard
> Doing maths

One day I had to do about 3 hours 30 minutes homework.

There is one thing they cannot take away from me and that is my happiness.

One teacher pulled my hair for singing.

I would like to get a mighty microphone so I could tell everyone.

There are bullies in the school trying to trip me up.

I think that everything comes apart in my hands like when I broke the phone and smash things.

Example 16

A letter written by an intelligent forty year old man.

Dear Jean

I hope this letter will help you to understand me better?

I was born in a place called Wrekonton which is in the North East of England .15 miles from Dushm city to the north .

I atendted three scools with little or no suckces but since having been having lessons with you I am fineding that your help is beging to give me som confidence in my self I am sorry if I have gives you the impreation that I have lost interest. I think that if I have my lesson on tape so as I can play them at will, I hope it will me to tern fasten

I have been doged all of my life with this problem now that I have found out the main problem to my not being able agust in the normal way I just hope and proey that some day in the not to fave distant fut her I will be able to fiend some happyness and stable acseptence in the comunity

But I must add that the harder I try some times th harder I fall I am what a lot of people call a (J arther). I would allso like to point out that some times my mined just blanks out in the time it takes me to go from one room to the nexed I gess the fact that I am dyslexic it has set the patern to my life to date I hope this garple is of serme uese so that you can help me help my self to do a Robert the Bource

Gillian is now sixteen years old and has recently taken her O level examinations. She hopes to go to Sixth Form College and eventually to University to read English. She was one of the lucky children who was assessed and given expert tuition. She describes dyslexia as she sees it.

"Allow me to give you a description of dyslexia from the inside.

It has taken me 15 years to form a conclusion of what life is like for me, not because I now see myself any differently but because I begin to realise how different "normal" people's mental processes are.

I am 15 and reasonably intelligent. My reading and spelling are good, in fact just as good (until under stress conditions) as my peers.

However, it seems that the 'normal' processes involved with reading, etc. are totally alien to me.

I have tried to put into words the process called reading as it happens to me. This is what happens.

1   *I must first ascertain in which direction the words flow, i.e., left to right.*

2   *Next, I have to make that direction mean something tangible (to me, the words left and right are meaningless and could easily be replaced with cup and saucer).*

3   *Having understood that instruction, I have to make the line "stand still".*

4   *In order to make the words "stand still", my mind divides into two parts.*

   I call the first "brute force" and it mentally restrains the word from jumping about and changing, i.e. "was" to "saw".

5   *The second half then comes into play and reads what the first half is restraining. My friend "brute force" also has to restrain the letters which also move about within my mind.*

6   *Now the problems begin.*

   If my reading is correct, the sentence means something. Occasionally, when I am tired, or only half concentrating, "brute force" allows the words to slip, and their meaning alters.

   If the sentence is garbled and makes no sense, I begin again. However, the sentence does often read sensibly, but not correctly. "I saw a cow" does not mean "I was a cow".

Reading is not the only problem. Directional instructions are impossible to comprehend.

I put it down to this:

If as a child your image was unstable and you are learning the difference between top and bottom, correct interpretation depends on whether your image was the right way up to begin with. Being bilateral my physical interpretation of left and right are identical. The words mean nothing. Physically I know exactly in which direction I am turning. However, I may not choose the correct title for that direction. In other words, I say left and mean your interpretation of the word right. Written directions are impossible to follow as, firstly, the words can be read incorrectly, and my idea of bottom left could be your idea of top right. The same applies to telling the time which until recently, (thanks to the patient teachings of a fellow dyslexic) seemed unattainable.

My complaint is that I was so often labelled "thick", when really I am fairly bright. Only because my mind works logically, often drawing the wrong conclusions.

Take the alphabet. Until recently I took the instruction "re-arrange these words in A B C order" to mean literally put the letters of the word into alphabetical order, e.g. danger = a d e g n r. What the instruction actually means is put this word, as it is, into a list of words which are in alphabetical order. I could not understand how dictionaries contained complete intelligible words when they were apparently in "alphabetical order".

It isn't really stupidity, merely misconception, or a different interpretation.

I am not saying that is what dyslexia is for all dyslexics. Indeed, many dyslexics whom I know have totally dissimilar problems. But there is usually one link which remains throughout. The inability to extract the jumbled word inside the mind and write it intelligibly.

Somewhere between seeing, storing in the memory and using the word again, something goes wrong. I only wish someone knew what."

Gillian

USEFUL ADDRESSES

British Dyslexia Association
98 London Rd., Reading, Berks. RG1 5AU

The Dyslexia Institute
133 Gresham Road, Staines, Middlesex TW18 2AJ

The Helen Arkell Dyslexia Centre
Frensham, Farnham, Surrey GU10 3BW

The National Hospital
Queen Square, London WC1

The Westminster Children's Hospital
London SW1P NS

St. Bartholomew's Hospital
West Wing, West Smithfield EC1A 7BE

Guy's Hospital
St. Thomas Street, London SE1

St. Thomas' Hospital
Lambeth Palace Road, London SE1

Charing Cross Hospital
Fulham Palace Road, London W6

The Belgrave Hospital
The Wilfred Sheldon Paediatric Assessment Centre
Offley Road, London SW9

Education Assessment and Guidance Service
235 Staines Road, Laleham, Middlesex TW18 2RS

Occupational Guidance Unit
Hythe House, 200 Shepherds Bush Road, London W6 7NR

FURTHER READING

Assessment and Teaching of Dyslexic Children	Published by I.C.A.A.
Dyslexia — Introduction	A Dyslexic's Eye View
All available from	The Problem of Reading
The Helen Arkell Dyslexia Centre	The Problem of Spelling
	The Problem of Handwriting
	Speech Therapy and the Dyslexic
	Motivation
	The Problems of Sequencing and Orientation
	Books for the Dyslexic
Diagnosis in the Classroom	by Gill Cotterell
	Available from L.D.A.
The Dyslexic Child	by MacDonald Critchley
Dyslexia Defined	by MacDonald Critchley
On Helping the Dyslexic Child	by Professor Miles
More Help for the Dyslexic Child	by Professor Miles
The Dyslexic Child	by Professor Miles
Concessions for Dyslexic Candidates in GCE & CSE Examinations	Available from The Dyslexia Insitute, 133 Gresham Road, Staines

USEFUL TEACHING MATERIALS

Dyslexia — A Language Training Course for Teachers and Learners	by Kathleen Hickey Obtainable from Bath Educational Publishers
A Remedial Approach to the Teaching of Reading, Spelling and Writing	by V.J. Wight Boycott Available from 'The Chesteine', High Street, Milverton, Somerset TA4 1LW
Alpha to Omega	by Hornsby & Shear Available from Bath Educational Publishers
Learn to Spell	by W.D. Wright. Pub. J. Nesbet
Read, Write and Spell Books 1, 2, 3 & 4	by Julia Leech and Gillian Nettle Pub. Heinemann Educational Available from Bath Educational Publishers

Read Write and Spell Books 1, 2, 3 & 4	by Julia Leech and Gillian Nettle Heinemann Education Books Ltd. 48 Charles St., London W1X 8AN
Logical Spelling	by B.V. Allen. Pub. Collins
Spelling Patterns	by B.V. Allen. Pub. Collins
Edith Norrie Letter Case	Available from The Helen Arkell Dyslexia Centre
Signposts to Spelling	by Joy Pollock Available from Bath Educational Publishers
The Pergamon Dictionary of Perfect Spelling	Wheaton & Co. Ltd.
Spellbound	by Elsie T. Rak Available from Bath Educational Publishers
Dictionary of Confusibles	by G.A. Owen Available from James Brodie Ltd., Brodie House, Queen Square, Bath
Thorndyke Junior Illustrated Dictionary	London University Press
Walkers Rhyming Dictionary	Routledge & Kegan Paul
Catalogue for much useful apparatus	Learning Development Aids, Duke St., Wisbech, Cambs. (Most items also available from Bath Educational Publishers)
Blank Playing Cards	Available from Bath Educational Publishers
Wooden Alphabet Letters	Galt and Co., Brookfields Road, Cheadle, Cheshire
Tactiles	Available from 66 Combemartin Road, Southfields, London SW18 5PR
Tutorpack Machine and programmes	Packman Research Ltd., Twyford, Berks.
Language Worksheets	Fordigraph, Ofrex House, London

Philograph Publications Ltd.   Northway, Andover, Hampshire
Visual Perceptual Materials   MacMillan Education Ltd.
Michegan Tracking Programme   Ann Arbor

Most of the above are available either from stock or to order from
Bath Educational Publishers Ltd., 7 Walcot Buildings, London Road,
Bath, BA1 6AD, who will send their catalogue on request.

BRITISH DYSLEXIA ASSOCIATION

```
British Dyslexia Association
98 London Road
Reading
Berkshire
RG1 5AU
Tel: 0734 668271/2
```

LOCAL ASSOCIATIONS

*Areas in which Dyslexia Associations are located, secretaries change
from time to time , please contact British Dyslexia Association
(address above) for latest information.*

BARNSLEY	LANCASHIRE
BATH	LINCS & HUMBERSIDE
BEDFORD	LONDON
BERKSHIRE	MERTON
BIRMINGHAM	MIDLANDS
BOLTON & DISTRICT	NEWCASTLE (NORTH EAST)
BUCKS (NORTH)	NORTHERN IRELAND
BUCKS & BERKS (SOUTH)	NOTTS
CAMBRIDGE	OXFORDSHIRE
CHESHIRE	PLYMOUTH
CORNWALL	RICHMOND UPON THAMES
CROYDON	SELBY
CUMBRIA (SOUTH)	SHEFFIELD
DERBY	SHROPSHIRE
DEVON	SOUTHPORT & DISTRICT
DORSET	STAFFORD (NORTH)
ESSEX	SURREY (NORTH)
ESSEX (SOUTHEND)	SURREY (WEST)

GLOUCESTER
GWYNEDD
HAMPSHIRE
HARROGATE
HEREFORD & WORCS
HERTS
JERSEY & CHANNEL ISLANDS
KENT (CENTRAL)
KENT (NORTH)

SURREY (SOUTH EAST)
SUSSEX (EAST)
SUSSEX (WEST)
WAKEFIELD
WALES (SOUTH)
WARWICKSHIRE
WAVENEY VALLEY
WIRRAL

AREAS OF INTEREST

BRIDGEWATER
CLWYD (NORTH WALES)
LEICESTER

LEEDS & DISTRICT
LIVERPOOL

MIDDLESEX
PETERBOROUGH
WALSALL

NON-AFFILIATED ASSOCIATIONS

SWINDON   SALISBURY (WILTS)   NORTH HUMBERSIDE

OTHER ORGANISATIONS

SCOTTISH DYSLEXIA ASSOCIATION
DYSLEXIA ASSOCIATION OF IRELAND